GIMME A BREAK!

GIMME A BREAK!

Warner Wolf
with
William Taaffe

McGRAW-HILL BOOK COMPANY
New York San Francisco St. Louis Toronto Mexico

Printed in the United States of America.

1 2 3 4 5 6 7 8 9 D O C D O C 8 7 6 5 4 3

ISBN 0-07-071537-8

Library of Congress Cataloging in Publication Data

Wolf, Warner.
Gimme a break!
1. Sports—Anecdotes, facetiae, satire, etc.
2. Television and sports—Anecdotes, facetiae, satire, etc. I. Taaffe, William. II. Title.
GV707.W64 1983 796'.0207 83-9810
ISBN 0-07-071537-8

Book design by Roberta Rezk

Acknowledgments

I'd like to thank all the engineers, technicians, and cameramen and-women who over the years have contributed to each success I have enjoyed on the air.

Thanks to my sports producers at WCBS-TV—Carmine Cincotta (with whom I've worked since 1976), Cliff Gelb, Andy Jones, and Doug Grabiner—and to all the young interns who helped us watch thousands of ball games over the years.

A special thanks to all the late-night videotape editors I have been fortunate to have, including Jimmy Holder, Vinnie Collica, Jo Ellen Farina, Don Dotson, and Tony DiGiovanni, who have spent many a long night beyond the call of duty to give me the best sports videotape possible.

I am grateful to Mrs. Donna Taaffe, who patiently typed this manuscript more than once.

And thanks to the Lord for giving me the tools and the ability to have a successful career in this business.

Contents

Prologue

Ever since I can remember, I wanted to be a sportscaster. While other guys wanted to become dentists, doctors, lawyers, policemen, or go into their fathers' businesses, I knew that I'd be in sports. As far back as the sixth grade, I can remember reading sports books and magazines, listening to ball games on the radio and going to the ball park. I was constantly talking sports. It was always my dream . . . someday to be a sportscaster.

By making my living as a sportscaster on radio and TV for the past twenty-two years, I have been fortunate enough, through the grace of God, to have that dream fulfilled.

This story is about that dream, the ups and downs in a career that began April Fool's Day, 1961. It's about how you must keep going, even after the disappointments and failures, never losing that drive and self-confidence.

For the past seven and a half years I have been blessed by working in the world's number one radio-TV market, New York City. With all respect to the other great markets in the world, there is no experience like living and working in New York.

For the past three and a half years I have worked for WCBS-TV, Channel 2, New York. During the four years before, I was with WABC-TV, Channel 7, New York. And for the past year and a half, I have also been employed by the *CBS Morning News*, where I appear every Friday morning at 7:45. To me, I have the best of both worlds: locally, ten times a week, Monday through Friday, broadcasting to a potential twelve million people in the New York City area, and once a week, on the *Morning News*, broadcasting to the entire country.

I now have what I refer to as a "Non-Aggravation Contract" and peace of mind. The WCBS and CBS management has shown complete confidence in me by giving me a free hand in the selection of my material. A higher compliment could not be paid to one on the air.

My dream is fulfilled and my life is complete. But it wasn't always like that. I'd like to tell that story.

1

Opening Lines

BOOM!

Behind his desk in the Supreme Court for the County of New York, Justice Burton S. Sherman pounded his gavel. The trial was about to begin. May 29, 1980. BOOM! *Ladies and gentlemen, American Broadcasting Companies, Inc., against Warner Wolf.* I can still hear the gavel. One of the biggest corporations in America suing me, Warner Wolf. They accused me of breaching my contract, when in fact my contract had expired March 6, 1980. Come on, man, gimme a break! I just want to go on TV and do the sports every night and then go home to my wife and kids.

When the gavel came down I started looking around the courtroom. All I saw were eyes, hands, file folders, and papers. Everybody had papers. I'll tell you this: If you can avoid going on trial, avoid it. It is not what you see on TV. It's no fun at all. The other side's lawyers try to make you feel like a criminal.

"Isn't it true your name is Warner Wolf?" asked the ABC attorney—like that was a crime or something.

And, "Isn't it true you are currently employed by the American Broadcasting Companies, 1330 Avenue of the Americas, New York, New York?"

"Well, of course," I thought, "of course I am. Is that a crime?"

I couldn't get over the irony of this. Almost twenty years in the business, you work your way up to the top, you become the number one local sportscaster in the biggest city in the land (according to a *New York Daily News* poll), and this is what it comes down to—*American Broadcasting Companies against Warner Wolf.* Not even a sports story. I mean, a legal story. Something for the *Law Review*.

Back in the gallery were reporters from *Variety,* the *New York Post,* the *New York Daily News,* and *Newsday*. I started thinking about what I would have told 'em if I'd been able to talk at that particular time.

The first thing I would have said is this: Television is great on one hand, but sometimes bad news on the other. You can be an overwhelming success one year, and total failure the next.

In September 1979 my two-year contract at WABC was coming up for renewal. The exact month it was to expire was March 1980. I wanted to begin negotiations on a new contract several months ahead of time so my wife, children, and I could plan ahead. No problem, Channel 7 said. We met again in October and the general manager said he would get back to me in ten days. *Ten days*. Those words eventually were to become famous.

The next time we heard from him or any other representative of the station was in January. Three months and not a peep out of anyone. When they finally did make me an eleventh-hour offer, I told them it was too late. Their time had passed.

How we wound up in court that May 29 speaks volumes about ABC's motives. As Casey Stengel used to say, you can look it up. It's all there in the court record, New York County Clerk's Index No. 8959/80. First, ABC ignored my requests to negotiate a new contract. Then they signed a paper that we felt specifically allowed me to go elsewhere upon the conclusion of the contract. Finally, they sued me for breach of contract.

I was sitting there at the defense table with a lot of thoughts going through my mind. I figured, well, you just tell the court exactly what happened and have faith that the judge will see the truth. I was certain ABC was wrong and willing to go to court to prove I was right. This was one time I could have said "Boo, man!" or "Gimme a break!" and been absolutely justified.

My career at ABC was supposed to have proceeded without a ripple. Why should I have expected problems? Everything had worked for me in the past, right? Pikeville, Ky., Martinsburg, W. Va., Silver Spring, Md., Washington, D.C.—no problems. But the network taught me one of the most valuable lessons I'll ever learn: You can't really be a success in this business until you've failed. No way. Unless you've been at the bottom, you can never fully understand what it's like being at the top.

It's funny, but all through those early years, one part of me was satisfied with where I was and one part of me wanted something more. Even when things where going great in Washington, I'd say to myself, "Hey, this is great. This is it." But in the back of my mind I wanted to be on the network. New York was *the* place. When I started out in 1961, my father cut out a story about a radio news guy who had knocked around for fifteen years before he ever got to New York. I folded it up and tucked it in my wallet. Over the years, I got rid of wallets but I never threw out the clipping. I still had it fifteen years later when ABC hired me to come to New York. I kept it as a reminder. I knew someday I would make it.

You know how some people say that if you can start at the top, then start at the top? Forget it. You should start at the bottom and put in the years, otherwise you don't learn the business. Maybe other people can do it faster, but I was on radio eight years before ever getting on television. And it was seven more years before I got to New York.

I've got nothing against ex-athletes being on the air—some are great as analysts and some as play-by-play men because they have been down on the field. But you don't see many ex-athletes become sportscasters on the 6 p.m. and 11 p.m. news. The reason is they haven't learned the business. Come on, man, you've got to start on a small-town radio or television station just like the minor leagues. You've got to be a disc jockey. You've got to read the news when nobody's listening, like 6 o'clock on Sunday morning.

On small-town stations you do it all. You play your own records, operate your own dials, tear the news off the wire, and promote the local fair. My first break came when John Hays, the president of WTOP Radio and TV in Washington, took a liking to me. "Warner," he said, "you seem to know something about sports. We're starting a new format here called 'talk radio.' How would you like to have your own show?"

This led to television in 1969. I did play-by-play of the Washington Redskins, the old Washington Senators, the Washington Bullets, and University of Maryland football. I did the 6 and 11 o'clock news, plus a weekly sports highlight show. I started the "Boo of the Week." Pretty soon I was number one in Washington, according to a poll in the *Washington Post,* and my wife and I were invited to a state dinner at the White House.

When you come up in broadcasting, you're taught two things. One is the point about New York being the only place. And second, the ultimate in television is the network. So even though I was satisfied in Washington, when the networks began to call, I listened.

The first call was from the president of ABC Sports. Soon CBS and NBC got wind of ABC's interest and also started wooing me. That's how the networks work. If one network gives you the rush, they all do. Finally I gave in. ABC won. They seemed to show the most interest and they were the first who came knocking at my door. Therefore they had me. I went to New York.

For a while, ABC was great. They gave me some of the 1976 winter and summer Olympics. They put me on *Monday Night Baseball*. They made me the host of *Wide World of Sports* and the *College Football Scoreboard* show. And on the side, we worked out an agreement where I did the local sportscast on the 6 o'clock news for WABC–Channel 7, the network-owned station in New York. Here I was, Warner Wolf, the kid who used to sit in the bleachers at Griffith Stadium in Washington, playing from New York to Los Angeles. This was great. I'd be on local TV in New York, and I'd also be seen across the country on network TV.

Earlier, I had always felt at home working in Washington. After all, it *was* my home. I had good press. I told them I was in the entertainment business and they understood. They knew that if Sonny

Jurgensen, for example, got in trouble for off-the-field activities, I wouldn't have it on my show. I'd let the news department cover it.

But when I went to the network, it was gloves off. The national press and the New York press bombed me. I remember one time a guy from *Sports Illustrated* absolutely killed me. I had done a Mets game against the Cardinals. Tom Seaver, who had a bad leg at the time, tagged up and went from second to third on a fly ball. "Seaver showed me something," I said. "He's got a bad leg and still he tags up and goes to third." The guy writes that Warner Wolf is astonished that Tom Seaver, a good base runner, can run 90 feet to third. Hey, the writer missed the point about the bad leg.

Another guy who bombed me was from the *Chicago Tribune*. After the final game of the American League playoffs in 1976, the one in which Chris Chambliss won the pennant for the Yankees with a homer in the bottom of the ninth, I was ordered to go into the losers' locker room and talk to the Royals' George Brett, who had tied the game with a three-run homer the inning before. The newspaper guy says I didn't ask the right questions and was too easy on Brett. Come on, Brett was crushed, you could see he was in tears. I couldn't believe what this guy wrote. Even my wife felt that one. She said, "This is a personal attack. You sure you never did something to this guy?"

Much later, in January 1982, after I had come over to WCBS–Channel 2 in New York, North Carolina played Alabama in the NCAA basketball playoffs. The game started at 8:30 p.m. EST. It just so happened, the CBS network carried the game, but decided to play it on a delayed basis in New York. Even though the game would be over, they decided not to show it until 11:30 p.m.

Well, that's their prerogative. Personally, as a sports fan, I wouldn't stay up till 2 a.m. to watch a game on a delayed basis, which in reality ended $2^1/_2$ hours before.

On my 11 p.m. sportscast, at approximately 11:15, I give the fourth-quarter score with three minutes to go. I tell them it's North Carolina by five points. Then, just as the newscast is signing off at 11:30, I put up a *card,* which says, "With :38 seconds to go, it's N.C. by 3 pts."

Well, the next week this writer from the *New York Post* really rips me. He says how dare I put up a score of a game which will be shown on a delayed basis, following the news. Calls me irresponsible. Never calls to ask me for an explanation, mind you. Just bombs me.

Here's how I feel:

Number one, it is my duty as a sportscaster to give the latest possible scores of all important games—keeping in mind, while I was giving the score at 11:15, that every other sportscaster in New York on the air at that time was doing the same thing.

Number two, for every one person who is going to stay up until 2 a.m. and watch a game which ended 2½ hours ago, there are ten people who will not wait up till 2 a.m. and who just want to know the score.

Number three, what the CBS sports network decides to do with a game is strictly their business, and has absolutely no effect or influence on what I do or say during my sportscast. I work for WCBS-TV, Channel 2, in New York City—not for CBS network sports.

In my mind, there was no decision to make. As a sportscaster, the latest possible score had to be given.

I was naive when I came to the network. I thought it was going to be the same there as it was at WTOP–Channel 9 in Washington. I thought I'd be able to say the same things as long as I was fair. It was a terrible lesson to learn. I didn't have half the freedom at the network that I had had on the 6 and 11 o'clock news. They had their own way of doing things. You either went along with them, or you lost out.

The thing that bothered me most was that they had scouted me for years on WTOP. They knew what I was like, they knew the reasons for my success in Washington. They had heard the "Boo of the Week," and they knew I was opinionated. So if they didn't want to go for my stuff, why hire me? Don't hire me and then try to change me.

By the start of the 1977 season, I was gone from the "A" game of *Monday Night Baseball* and was now a member of the "B" and "C" teams. That's the network equivalent of being sent down to the minor leagues. I got bounced off the *College Football Scoreboard* show after my second year. I began to get fewer and fewer *Wide World of Sports* assignments. When I did get them, they were of the target-diving-from-Fort Lauderdale variety.

The weirdest part of all was that until they relieved you from a show they would never tell you what was wrong. They would not call you in for a talk. You slowly became a nonperson. It was as though you had fallen out of favor in the Kremlin. It got to the point where I had nothing to do except the 6 o'clock sports at WABC–Channel 7. Here the network was paying me $150,000 a year not to use me. Except for a Ping-Pong tournament in England, and two baseball games, I had no assignments for eleven months.

I can honestly say that those eleven months—from April 1977 to March 1978—were one of the darkest periods of my life. Bad, man. I became hard to live with. I didn't feel good about myself. Even though I was under contract and it was perfectly legal, I was taking money for doing nothing.

Besides the support of my wife, the one thing that kept me going during these months was the slow realization that local television, not the network, was really the place for me.

When I first went to work for ABC, I signed a two-year *network* contract. This contract expired in March 1978. Not wanting to do any more Ping-Pong on national TV, I signed instead with WABC–Channel 7 to handle both the 6 and 11 o'clock news. I was back to *local* television completely. It was the same thing I had done in Washington, except now I was in the number one television market—and fortunately for me, New Yorkers really seemed to like my style.

First, let me tell you the terrific side of going back to local. The moment you know you've made it is when the guy on the street begins to holler at you. I guess I make people laugh a lot, so they're usually in a good humor. "Hey, how ya' doin', Warner?" "Hey, let's go to the videotape!" Out of car windows, trucks, everywhere. It's a nice feeling to walk on the street in New York and people wave or shake your hand, that's when you know you've made it. It makes you feel like this is your city.

Why do people react this way? I have a few ideas.

First of all, I am an entertainer. As soon as your face appears regularly on the screen, you become a performer whether you like it or not. I'm amazed at some people in the TV business who resent that. They want to call themselves strictly journalists and not performers. Hey, that's OK—but TV is still show business. Go with it right out front.

Another thing is humor. I'm no judge, but I think too many guys take sports too seriously. Come on, it's games, let's have some humor in here. As long as the humor is in good taste, you're OK.

One principle I've always followed is I've never made fun of what happens to guys off the field. As I tell all news directors, if you want to hear a gossip columnist, then go listen to a Rona Barrett. I think sports and weather are the only parts of a newscast where you can get away from the wars, the murders, the bank robberies, and the gloom. Sports and weather. They're like comedy relief.

Also, be simple. Get right to the point. It seems to me too many guys on the air—not only on the air but in life—take too long to get to the point. Don't give me a preface and an index. Just say what you want to say. You want to say the baseball season starts too early and ends too late? Then say it. Just like that. A lot of guys try to be fancy and flowery. That's baloney! Sports fans don't care about being fancy. Just tell 'em what happened.

I try to make out like I'm talking to a guy right across from me in a bar. In my opinion a sportscaster has got to be talking to the doorman, he's got to be talking to the sanitation man, he's got to be talking to the taxi driver and the bartender. The majority of your audience is made up of everyday, down-to-earth people.

People ask me how I know what to put on the air. I know because I'm an average person who knows what the average person wants to see. Too many guys don't know what the average person wants to see or hear. If you're in commercial television, you've got to communicate with the masses.

Every now and then you hear about a television performer wanting to be a recluse. I can't understand that. People ask me if I enjoy the attention. Are you kidding? It's great. Terrific. If I didn't get it, I'd say, "Uh-oh, they're not watching." I was walking down the street in New York a few years ago and I saw Buddy Rich, the great drummer, coming my way. I'm usually shy around strangers. As we got closer Buddy Rich stopped me. ''Warner Wolf, how ya' doin'?'' he said, sticking out his hand. ''Warner Wolf,'' he said, ''yeah, I watch you all the time.'' Boy, Buddy Rich shaking my hand? This was a thrill.

However, another time I saw Robert Duval, the great character actor, standing on the corner of 63rd and Broadway. I went up to him and told him how much I admired his work. He thanked me, and I asked him, ''Didn't you live in Arlington or Alexandria, Virginia?''

''Yeah. Sure did,'' he said.

''I thought so. Well, I'm Warner Wolf. You know me. Channel 9? WTOP? Did the sports in Washington ten years?''

Duval looked at me with a mystified expression. ''No, can't say I remember.''

''Channel 9?'' I asked. ''You know, Max Robinson, Gordon Peterson, and the Eyewitness News Team?''

''Nope, I just can't seem to recall,'' he said. ''But then, I've been up here in New York for some time, now, so maybe that explains it.

''By the way, Mr. Wolf, what do you do with yourself now?''

Unbelievable. A double-header. Shot down twice by one person. He didn't remember me in Washington and he's never seen me in New York. But if you want the truth, being disappointed like this is good for you now and then. It's hard to stay humble if you are on television. You have to make a conscious effort to remember that just because you're on TV, you're not any different from the next guy. You're still only a person. And, in the end, we're all the same anyway.

2

Early Days, or, Life with Father

Throughout my life there was one person who walked with me step by step. He was my father, Jack Wolf. He was the greatest man I ever knew.

He died at age 56, November 14, 1965, a few months after I started at my first major station—WTOP Radio in Washington, D.C. You have to realize that we were much closer than most fathers and sons. Like brothers, actually. With the exception of Pikeville, Ky., and Martinsburg, W. Va., he heard every broadcast I ever did. No matter what the hour, he listened. He would call the moment the show was done.

Now when I talk about being an entertainer on television and giving people some humor, I have to put in a plug for my mother and father. That's where I got it from. They had me on November 11, 1937. They had been in vaudeville. He was a musician and a comedian and she was a dancer. I was their only child. They played the famed Palladium in London. They played the Palace Theater in New York. In 1932 they played in *Crazy Quilt,* a Billy Rose Broadway show with the legendary Fanny Brice.

My father was more than just a routine vaudeville performer. He, my cousin "Mousy" Garner, and another man named Dick Hakins made up "The Gentle Maniacs," the slapstick group that succeeded "The Three Stooges" on the stage. They were fairly well known. Actually, the producer, Ted Healy, referred to the Maniacs as "Healy's Stooges" even though the original three—Curly, Mo, and Larry, and later Shemp —had left vaudeville for the movies.

My father used to tell me stories about Red Skelton, who was penniless at that time and not well known. "Hey, this guy's funny, he can do pantomime, he's gonna be good," my father used to say. My father said he took Red under his wing, sometimes paying Red's hotel bill and buying him a meal or two. One time, when Red was broke and had no idea where his next meal was coming from, my father said he took Red to a Chinese restaurant. You know how they say you can eat Chinese food and still be hungry an hour later? Well, Red went in and instead of ordering Chinese food, he orders bacon and eggs. He wanted a meal that would stick to his stomach.

With the decline in vaudeville, my parents decided to get out of show business, settle in Washington, D.C., and raise a family. My father owned an amusement arcade at 9th and D streets next to the Gayety Burlesque Theater. He also was a liquor salesman and later worked for Milton Kronheim, who had a good portion of the market in the city. My father was soft-sell all the way. He was a gentle man. But I tell you what, he worked hard. I'd come home and he'd be there, poring over his accounts, thinking of ways to sell more orders. He never beat people over the head on why they should buy from him, but he would come up with special offers and fancy displays. He always managed to be a step ahead.

Some people have the notion that Warner Wolf must be a stage name. But Warner Wolf is the name on the birth certificate. Warner William Wolf.

As far as family background goes, I have a minor claim to presidential history. I'm one of the few living Jewish relatives of Abraham Lincoln. My grandmother on my mother's side was Lilah Hanks, a cousin of Nancy Hanks, Lincoln's mother.

On my father's side of the family, my grandfather worked until he was 85. He used to make change in the amusement arcade my father owned next to the burlesque house. He was around all the time. Grandpa Charlie Wolf. He was born in South Africa and lived in England for a while before coming to the States. Originally his name was Levy. His father was a diamond merchant who was killed on a safari and robbed of his jewels. Charlie's mother then married a man named William Wolf and moved to London, England.

For me, I guess, the moral of the story is that my name really could be Warner Levy. To find out what happened I've written the South African department of family trees and asked some questions. "Why did Charlie Wolf change his name from Charlie Levy?" Usually, when a child's parents divorce and the mother remarries, the child keeps the father's name, unless the kid is adopted. That wasn't the case with Charlie. As of this date, I've had no response.

Another strange thing about my family tree is that everybody seems to have been born on a national holiday. My father was born on the Fourth of July and my mother was born on Labor Day. They were married on Thanksgiving. I was born on Armistice Day, November 11, which is now called Veterans Day. And my youngest daughter, Shayna—that's Yiddish for "beautiful"—was born on Memorial Day.

When you're an only child, you spend a lot of time with your parents. They are your pals. They are the first people you think of doing things with. You pick up expressions and ideas from them the way other kids pick up things from their own age group.

My father and I were a team. We used to take the streetcar from our house near Georgia Avenue and Sheridan Street down to old Griffith Stadium. It took about twenty-five minutes and cost 20 cents. Every Sunday when the Senators were home, we went out. We used to carry chair backs that we would attach to the wooden planks in the bleachers. When you came down the hill on the streetcar, you would know you were getting close because you could see the light towers over the red brick row houses.

What a park that was. It had a smell of hot dog mustard and old cigars. Kids would make loud sounds by stomping on paper cups just to hear the "pop!" The huge outfield, with brilliant green grass. The big W's on the Senators' white uniforms. The clock in back of the bleachers. If you were growing up in Washington, you didn't care about Yankee Stadium. This was it, man—Griffith Stadium!

The bleachers ran from left field to right-center—a long bleachers. It was 405 feet to left field and 420 feet to straightaway center. Before the beer garden was erected to shorten the distance in the mid-1950s, you could go to five straight games and never see a home run into the left field stands—maybe over the right field wall, but not into the left field bleachers. That's why Mickey Mantle's shot of 565 feet over the left-center field bleachers off Chuck Stobbs in April 1953 was so much more amazing. The ball actually clipped the lower righthand corner of the National Bohemian Beer sign, located on top of the last row of the bleachers, before going out of the stadium. The ball landed in a back yard behind the stadium and was eventually retrieved by Yankee Press Attaché Red Patterson, after paying a youngster, who had reached the ball first, five dollars for it. Since it was 460 feet from home plate to the last row of bleachers and considering the last row of the bleachers was 55 feet high, plus another 5 feet high where Mantle's ball nicked the scoreboard, Patterson estimated by the time Mantle's shot reached the back yard the ball had traveled 565 feet—still the longest official home run in major league history. It was also the first of what we now commonly refer to as "The Tape Measure Homerun."

The question people have always asked is, "How much farther would Mantle's ball have gone, had it not hit the beer sign before leaving the stadium? Six hundred feet—650—who knows?"

Sitting in the bleachers was a great deal. A ball game and a suntan for only 75 cents—and what characters they had there! There was only one place for my father and me—the bleachers!

During doubleheaders, the same guy used to walk around the bleachers saying over and over again, "Best buy in town, doubleheader, thirty-seven and a half cents a game!"

Another guy, in the eighth inning of every game, would suddenly run up to the railing in front of the bleachers and shout, "Knock eeet off! Knock eeet off! Nothing on it but the cover!" You could set your watch by this guy! Eighth inning, every game. Nobody knew what he meant, but we would all give him a hand. Between innings another guy used to yell, ''Open the gates! Open the gates!'' No one knew what he meant, but it was great.

My father and I saw some weird things from those bleachers. We used to talk to the outfielders. One time Camilo Pascual struck out Jungle Jim Rivera of the White Sox on a slow curve. Rivera looked so bad that he had completed his swing only to find out the pitch was still coming—or at least that's the way it looked from the bleachers.

So with the third out for the White Sox and the inning over, Rivera starts running out to the outfield. ''Boo! Boo!'' we're yelling. We're having a great time, really laying it on him, waving our hands and telling him he should go back to the minors. ''Hey, Jungle! Boo! Boo! You really looked bad, Jungle! You really looked bad!''

Jungle Jim waits for the crowd to subside. Finally he turns around and looks up, shakes his head and says, ''I never could hit well against a last-place team.''

The smartest play we ever saw was by Jim Piersall, the Red Sox center fielder. He did something in a night game against the Senators that my father and I talked about for years. It still ranks as the most quick-witted move I've seen.

Here's the scene: The score is tied, bottom of the ninth, the Senators have a man on first with two out and Pete Runnels at the plate. Runnels hits a line drive to right-center field. My father and I are sitting in the bleachers. The ball is coming straight toward the bull pen, almost in front of us. This is the bull pen Calvin Griffith installed in the late 1950s. It was surrounded by a low fence about four feet high. If you hit a ball into the bull pen on the fly, it was a home run. If it bounced in, it was a ground-rule double.

Now you have to realize this happens in a flash. Piersall runs toward the fence—he used to get a great jump on the ball—and catches up to it on one bounce in front of the bull pen with his back to the plate. My father and I now are facing Piersall. We have a perfect view of what's happening. As the ball bounces off the grass, Piersall pushes the ball into the bull pen. The winning run was already rounding third and the game was going to be over because Runnels's ball would still be in play, but Piersall flicks the ball into the bull pen. It becomes only a ground-rule double and the winning run has to come back to third.

Unbelievable. The guy was able to think quickly enough to push the ball in instead of letting it bounce off the bull pen wall. Well, the second-base umpire, Jim Rice, runs out, Piersall points to the ball in the bull pen, the umpire says, "You're right! Ground rule double," and waves the runner back to third. The Washington pitchers in the bull pen are going crazy and telling Rice that Piersall *pushed* the ball in. Three thousand people in the bleachers are yelling, "He pushed it in! He pushed it in!"

Rice says, "No way. Runners at second and third, play ball!" Sure enough, the next batter flies out, the game goes into extra innings, and the Red Sox win in the tenth.

We yelled at Piersall in the bottom of the ninth and again in the bottom of the tenth. Half the park was on him. "Piersall, you bum," we yelled, "you pushed it in! You pushed it in!" You know what he did? He turned around and gave us the biggest smile you've ever seen. He was admitting it and he was loving it. It was like he was sharing his secret with us.

The big thing with my father was the lessons he gave me. He taught them by example, not by punishment. I don't think I realized how much of an influence he had on me until after he was gone. He died too young —he was 56. I learned to appreciate him more later. When I started doing *Monday Night Baseball* on ABC, there were times I would catch myself. "Wow," I'd say, "wouldn't it be something if he were here? We'd be going around the country, seeing the parks, doing these games together . . ." I always had the feeling, if only he could see me now. Still have it, in fact. But he knows. I believe he's up there. I'm sure he's seen all the stuff I've ever done.

I suppose the thing I never fully appreciated while he was living was his finely developed sense of right and wrong. "You know, Mensch," he'd say, using the Yiddish word for man, "it's too bad in life you can't learn from my mistakes without having to make them yourself. You see, I already know what the result's going to be. But you're going to have to find out for yourself, even though I can tell you they're wrong in advance."

The guy was almost always right. I think he must have thought things through. He always had ethical lessons. You should always be humble, he said. You've got to be as nice to the doorman as you are to your boss. "See that guy? He's a human," he'd say. "Just because his job might not pay as much as yours, that doesn't mean a thing."

Because of their levity, my mother and father were always making a joke of something—you never thought of the word "stern" for my parents. But deep down, they were firm. My biggest fear was not in doing something wrong but in disappointing my father. I couldn't have a worse punishment than if he said, "Son, you've let me down." Wow, to me that was devastating. He had these shining principles you wanted to follow. We always went to High Holy Day services. We believed in God. But he never hit you over the head with it and he never talked about himself much.

Humor was one of the talents he left me. That and just having a knack for communicating directly. The two of us would sit there in the living room and watch live television shows that were supposed to be serious, but sometimes were funny.

Once we were watching *Playhouse 90*—a big show in those days—and there was a drama about this pioneer woman who was supposed to be alone, sitting in a chair in her kitchen, 80 miles from the nearest town. The play called for a fire to break out and she was supposed to put it out with a bucket of water. But they forgot to put a bucket on stage. All of a sudden we see this stagehand tiptoeing over to the fireplace. They do a close-up of her face, but you can see the stagehand in the background. He puts a water bucket down and tiptoes off. Hilarious! It's a live show, right? Here's this old lady all alone, who's supposed to be in the middle of nowhere and a stagehand brings her the water. We thought it was one of the funniest things we had ever seen.

A few years later, though, there was a live television commercial that beat it. John Cameron Swayze for Timex wristwatches. If you are old enough to have watched television in the 1950s, you may have seen it. The commercial called for Swayze to first remove his watch. "I'm going to show you what I did today," he'd say. "I put this Timex watch on this machine [he'd tape the watch to a boat propellor], lowered it into the water [he'd lower the propellor into a clear tank], and turned the switch! You'll never have a watch that will undergo *this* kind of test!''

After the propellor churned around for a while, Swayze would cut the switch, take the watch out, and put it to his ear. Then his face would light up and the camera would zoom in on the watch. ''Still running!'' he'd announce triumphantly, motioning the cameras to come in for a close look at the second hand.

The great thing about Swayze, who was also a newscaster, is he had a deep authoritative voice. Well, this one night he puts the watch in the tank to show you how durable it is. The propellor goes around and around. Finally he says, ''And now I'm going to turn off the motor and put my hand in the water!'' As he was doing it, you could see that the motor had chewed up the watch. No way was he going to get it out. You could see it hanging off the propellor blade, various parts of it sticking out. We fell on the floor, it was so funny. The machine had killed it—absolutely murdered the watch. Swayze stares at the camera, pauses, and then says, ''Well, it worked this morning.'' That was it. End of commercial.

Stuff like that was great. We'd always make fun of situations. Not to ridicule people—but hey, you make a hilarious mistake like that, you've got to laugh. But you've also got to be sensitive. My father had a great phrase. He used to say, ''If you can't laugh at yourself, you don't have a right to laugh at anybody else.'' Also, ''Take your work seriously but don't take yourself seriously.''

You can see that my father was not only my friend but my number one advisor and critic. He'd call up after each show or each newscast. ''Hey, you really emphasized that word. That was good,'' he'd say. Or, ''That sentence was too long'' or ''You mumbled that word.'' Every night without fail. We used to say he was my unofficial agent. I was on the radio at American University—a tiny station that could only be heard in certain parts of Washington—and he would drive around campus each night to get the best reception.

He would even come to my intramural softball games when I

was at George Washington University. He'd bring a folding chair and sit on the sideline. One time I was playing center field and this big guy hits a ball what seemed like then 300 feet, way over my head. (Although I wasn't much of a hitter, as a fielder, I'd always get a good jump on the ball.) I ran back, back, back, and reached up and caught the ball. I felt like Piersall. It was the only time I saw my father actually stand up and applaud a catch. However, in that same game, something else occurred which was indicative of my father. Earlier in the game I messed up a fly ball and tossed my glove in the air in disgust. Bad attitude. You know what he did? He called me over to the sidelines, right in the middle of the game, in front of everybody, and told me that was bush league and he never wanted to see that again.

Another great influence in my life has been my wife, Sue. I met Sue in 1968, three years after my father died. I was representing WTOP at a ''Radio Day'' gala staged by the Ad Club of Washington. They had hired these two hostesses—one of whom was Miss D.C. in the Miss Universe contest—to walk the radio guys down the aisle. The girls would rotate to a different aisle each time. I knew I wanted Miss D.C. to walk me down, so I waited until she was coming back to the left aisle at the exact moment I was ready.

Her name was Sue. She was working for Cinderella, which was a finishing school for girls—makeup and stuff like that. I called her that afternoon, and we went to a place on Connecticut Avenue a few nights later. They had a piano and a set of drums, and I asked the owner if I could play the drums. I guess I thought I was being impressive. She thought I was crazy.

Years later, when I had no work to do at ABC network and was jotting down idle thoughts while contemplating my future, I wrote this about her: ''There's no doubt about it, your best friend is your wife.''

I guess I first knew my father was sick in early 1965, around the time I joined WTOP. He had cancer of the colon. For the longest time I never knew how bad it was, but it *was* bad. He had it for about a year. He had two operations. I remember on Father's Day he had just had one of the operations and was making a comeback, putting weight back on, talking about the future.

That was an illusion, however. He always had a suntan, so he always looked healthier than he was. He had dark skin anyway, and he always dressed well. He had a neat mustache. He was my size. I used to wear his clothes; he'd pass them down to me instead of buying new ones. You know, I never considered ourselves poor. We always ate well and lived comfortably. But I guess we never did extravagant things, so when he passed me down his clothes, I thought they were good clothes. I was happy to wear them.

In reality he was getting worse all the time. But I never thought he was going to die even though he was going downhill. And he wouldn't accept that either. It wasn't like today when everybody knows. You didn't ask, you didn't know, there weren't so many magazine articles about it, and you didn't see it on TV. It was probably harder on my mother than it was on him. She would have to give him shots. He was always in pain, and it got to her. She had a weak heart. After my father died, she lived seven more years, but in all honesty, she really died when he died. That was it for her. She was just going through the motions the last seven years of her life. I always felt that it was a blessing when she did die so they could be together again.

After he came home from the hospital the last time, he just couldn't get his old spark back. The flame had been extinguished. Since he was with me from the start of my career, you would have expected him to be excited when he first heard me do the sports on WTOP. TOP was a big station, 50,000 watts, clear channel, people could hear it from Maine to Florida. But he seemed nonchalant.

It wasn't until November 9, five days before he died, that I really knew how sick he was. I had been at the National Press Club for a luncheon and had my picture taken with Gene Tunney and Jack Dempsey. I stood right between them for the cameraman, as though I were an old friend. Now you've got to realize my father and I were lifelong fight fans. Just to be near these guys was a huge thrill. So I called him up full of excitement. Boy, was he going to rave over this. "Dad, you're not going to believe what happened today," I yelled. "Guess who I had my picture taken with? TUNNEY and DEMPSEY!"

I remember a small, faint voice came back on the other end of the line. He sounded tired and far away. ''Oh . . . Oh,'' he said slowly. ''Tunney and Dempsey. That's good.'' It was like nothing had registered. Wow, I thought, if he can't get excited about Tunney and Dempsey, the time must be close. I came home that afternoon, and you could see the resignation in his eyes. That's when I knew.

One of the last times we talked was on my twenty-eighth birthday, November 11. It was one of the most emotional conversations I ever had.

He was propped up in bed in his room. I went in to see him because there was one question that had been weighing on my mind. We talked a little bit, and then I got to the point. I told him I needed to know if I had been a good son.

He seemed surprised by it. ''Warner,'' he said, as though he needed to get my attention, ''yes. Of course you have.''

Then he began in his own distinctive manner to say good-bye. As you can see, I loved him more than I can say. It broke my heart to listen.

''Warner,'' he said, ''I don't think I have it in me to make it.''

It was the first time he had ever said that. He had always fought it. Even when he had down periods, he always had said he was going to beat it. I didn't know what I should say.

''Ah, go on, Dad,'' I finally replied. ''Don't give me that.''

''Nah, I'm not going to make it, Warner. But this is your birthday. At least I waited until today. By the way, let me tell you something: This is the only time in our lives that I will be exactly twice as old as you.''

He died three days later. He had gone into a coma the day before. We tried to talk to him but there was no response. I'll never forget what it was like. The second before he died, he rose out of the bed with his arms extended, almost reaching out for something in front of him. Then he made a sound, fell back, and was gone. It was a Sunday morning. The Eagles beat the Redskins that day, 21–14. Preston Carpenter, a wide receiver the Redskins got from the Browns, broke his arm.

3

Good Ol' Radio

In the late 1940s, millions of American families would gather in the living room on Sunday night and turn on the radio. You listened to Jack Benny. He was a natural for radio because his humor depended to a great extent on timing. He would give you these silent pauses before delivering the punch line. You couldn't see anything, so you'd be hanging on his words, which made him all the more effective.

On Friday night it was *The FBI in Peace and War,* brought to you by Lava soap. At the sound of the tone the theme music welled up, the announcer introduced the night's episode, and then they'd cut to the Lava jingle. High note, low note, all the way through. "L–A–V–A, L–A–V–A." The three of us—Mom, Dad, and I—sat on the living room floor next to the stand-up radio, listening to one show after another. This was it—*radio!* There *was* no television. We sat there and stared at each other with excitement in our eyes. You didn't need television. You could use your imagination for how people looked.

I was born in 1937 and radio was half my life. A day did not go by in which I didn't dream what it would be like in that studio sitting behind the microphone, my voice going out over the cities.

We used to listen to *Gangbusters,* brought to you by Sloan's Liniment *Jack Armstrong, the All-American Boy; Grand Central Station,* which used to be on Sunday. We heard *Captain Midnight*;

The Shadow with Blue Coal as the sponsor; *Inner Sanctum,* where you heard the door squeak.

They used to have a game called *Quick as a Flash,* where you could play detective at home. Somebody would tell the story of a murder and drop just enough clues for you to figure out the killer by the process of deduction. The idea was to determine the murderer before the panelists in the studio could press their buzzers. They were real pros at it. They'd try to beat you to the punch and say, "I've got it! I've got it! The killer has got to be the maid because she was in the kitchen and it was a Tuesday and the kitchen is closed on Tuesday." If they were wrong, they were out of the game and you'd still have a chance.

I would sit beside the radio every night. Radio had great names—*The Green Hornet, Suspense, Mr. Keen, Tracer of Lost Persons, Amos 'n' Andy, Fibber McGee and Molly, Let's Pretend.* It was an age where you invented things with your mind. Other kids wanted to be sports stars or actors. All I wanted was to be on radio. Let me on! From the time I was 6 or 7 this was the only thing. Radio! RADIO! There was no television, so radio was the greatest medium there was. You woke up to it and went to bed with it.

I realize now that radio was one of the things that lured me into sports. Even before the end of World War II—I was 7—my father and I would listen to the *Friday Night Fights,* 10 to 11 o'clock, Don Dunphy doing the announcing. It became a ritual with us. We scored the fights from the sound of Dunphy's voice, which obviously was different than scoring it by sight. But Dunphy was great. Because of his delivery we would usually come out right. They scored by rounds with a supplementary point system in case of a draw. Not only would we have the winner, but we'd have either the two judges or the ref right on the nose, round for round. Radio made boxing come alive for me. It was the number one sport of my childhood. I'd always buy the *Ring Magazine* and read it on the way home from school. By the time I was 7 I had memorized every heavyweight champion from John L. Sullivan to Joe Louis.

Baseball could not compete with boxing in our house, but radio eventually hooked me on that as well. We had a porch in front of our place. When the Senators were on the road, my father and I used to sit on the porch, watch the traffic go by, and listen to Sunday doubleheaders from places like Yankee Stadium in New York, Comiskey Park in Chicago, and Briggs Stadium in Detroit. I had never seen these parks, but I could picture them from the radio. Yankee Stadium with its three decks. They said the sun was brightest in left field. I could see the haze and anticipate the sun. DiMaggio hitting a fly ball to Gil Coan in left, Coan putting down his sunglasses and making the catch.

Baseball on radio was unbelievably vivid. The grass was greener, the ball was whiter. You had to concentrate more with radio. You had to picture the sights in your mind.

The radio play-by-play guys used to be institutions. Where in television today, for example, would you find a guy like Arch McDonald? He used to re-create Senators' road games off the ticker tape, making believe the game was happening live when in reality he was simply reading the ticker, which was a couple of minutes old. He was great. He had a raspy, kind of gravelly voice, and he sounded like he never smiled too much. So what if he made a few things up? He was descriptive, he was dramatic, and if the game was close you sat there enthralled. Arch McDonald, the guy was a master at his profession.

One thing I liked best about him was he had some kind of gong he used to hit in the studio every time someone got a base hit. A single was one gong, a double two gongs, a triple three gongs, and four gongs for a home run. Sometimes McDonald would tip off his announcement of a Senators' home run by using a pet expression just before the blow.

The Senators used to have a shortstop named Mark Christman. Let's say Christman hits a home run. McDonald would say, "Here comes the pitch, Christman meets the ball, and MEET MR. CHRISTMAN!" followed by four gongs: *Gongggg! Gongggg! Gongggg! Gongggg!*

Or: "Here comes the pitch—AND THERE IT GOES, MRS. MURPHY!" *Gongggg! Gongggg! Gongggg! Gongggg!* "A HOME RUN!" This was great stuff. Of course, you knew the ball was out of there the moment he said, ''There it goes, Mrs. Murphy!'' But that was the fun of the re-creation.

Or: ''Three and one pitch to Vernon. Here it comes and there it goes. A long drive to right-center.'' *Gonggg!* ''It's between 'em. It rolls to the wall! Vernon around first, on his way to second.'' *Gongggg!* ''DiMaggio up with the ball, Vernon's gonna try for three. The throw to third.'' *Gongggg!* ''Too late! Vernon's in with a triple.''

Also, McDonald had these memorable expressions. Such as, if Washington had men on base, he'd say, ''The Senators have ducks on the pond.'' Another one was whenever the Senators came up trailing in the bottom of the ninth, two outs, he'd refer to the last batter by saying, ''Here comes the last of the Mohicans.''

This was 1946, 1947. The Senators didn't televise games on a regular basis until later, and McDonald was still doing re-creations on radio a few years after that. You could actually hear the ''tick-a-tick-a-tick-a'' of the Western Union machine in the background. The ticker would start and stop with every pitch, but the machine would go wild when there was a lot of action. A lot of times, if the Senators had a rally going, you'd try to anticipate what was going to happen. If you kept hearing the ''tick-a-tick-a,'' that was great. It probably meant the rally was still going on. If it stopped all of a sudden, you'd say to yourself, ''Aw, geez. I guess Eddie Yost hit into a double play to end the inning.''

Sometimes McDonald would have to cover for the Western Union operator. Let's say McDonald just got a message that Yost doubled. He'd give Yost two gongs and have him sliding into second. But hold everything! The operator now tells McDonald the previous message is wrong! It's not a double for Yost, but a single.

McDonald would say, ''Now our receiver in St. Louis—*tick-a-tick-a*—tells us—*tick-a-tick-a-tick-a*—that Yost thought better of going to second and actually stopped at first. Apparently Eddie didn't want to take a chance trying for second on Zarilla's arm.''

Or: ''Our receiver in Chicago *now* tells us that Vernon's drive went *over* the wall and did not hit the top of the fence. So—'' *Gongggg! Gongggg! Gongggg! Gongggg!* ''CREDIT MICKEY WITH

A HOME RUN AND NOT A DOUBLE!" Covering for the operator's mistakes like this kept the re-creation going. Plus McDonald was just having fun. He knew it was only a game.

McDonald collapsed and died of a heart attack while on a train with the Redskins after broadcasting a Giants-Redskins game in October 1960. I'll never forget—I was in the Army at Fort Sam Houston, Texas, and my father sent me the clipping that old Arch had died.

Another guy I listened to without fail was Bill Stern. He had a show called *The Cavalcade of Sports,* brought to you by Colgate Palmolive. He used to come on every Friday night. Boy, was this guy ever dramatic. His stories would build and build until that schoolboy quarterback he was telling you about suddenly turned out to be Dwight D. Eisenhower or Douglas MacArthur. Just listening to him gave me a sense of show business. He was the world's greatest optimist, but it wasn't until years later that I learned he made up some of his material.

You've heard the line about Washington being first in war, first in peace, and last in the American League? Well, the punch line at least was true. The Senators were so bad you had to create your own entertainment to keep from getting bored. The last pennant they won was in 1933. They had a shot at another pennant in 1945 but Bingo Binks, an outfielder, forgot his sunglasses, dropped a ball in the sun, the last weekend of the season, and that was it. The Tigers beat out Washington by 1½ games. Into the pits for the next twenty-six years. There was never any hope for the first division, much less a pennant. The only thing that mattered was *this game,* to win *this game*.

I saw a game in which the Senators had runners on first and third, one out, last of the ninth, they're losing by one run. Stan Spence hits a fly ball deep to right-center, which will be caught, the runner on third will score after the catch, and the game is going to be tied. Right? Wrong! The guy on third has all day to tag up and trot home—which is exactly what he does with what he thinks will be the tying run. But the runner on first also decides to tag up and go to second. Of course, the throw goes to second, he's called out, and the guy on third is still trotting home. His run doesn't count! Ball game's over. Senators lose, 2–1. "Thanks for coming, folks," the public address announcer says, "and please come back tomorrow for the exciting conclusion of this home stand . . ."

It went on like that for years, until Calvin Griffith formed a nucleus of good players like Harmon Killebrew, Camilo Pascual, Pedro Ramos, Roy Sievers, Earl Battey, and Bob Allison. That's why it angered the fans so much when Griffith up and left for Minnesota after the 1960 season. These guys suddenly could play ball, and the fans figured, "Hey, where's the fairness here? We stuck with 'em when they were bad. Now we're seeing the light and you're pulling 'em out."

But it was fun while it lasted, and one of the reasons was the park. You were so close to the players you could tell what kind of chewing tobacco they were using. Camera day was every day. "C'mon, Clint, pose for a shot with Ramos over there!" That was it, you could talk to them, it was all on a human scale. But as soon as the new expansion Senators moved into D.C. Stadium (later RFK Stadium) in 1962, forget it, the place was like a mausoleum. You could call to a player with a megaphone and he wouldn't even hear you. Griffith Stadium was never like that. It was made by human beings, not defense contractors.

When Griffith began to bring in power hitters for old Griffith Stadium—Sievers, Killebrew, Jim Lemon—he was smart enough to bring in the fences. In front of the long bleacher wall from left field to right-center field, he put in a beer garden. People sat at the picnic tables waiting for Sievers to pop one. The idea was to see if the ball could hit your cup. Whenever Sievers caught hold of one, everybody would hop up from the tables and start cheering and pointing at the beer so the ball knew where to go. "In my beer!" they'd yell. "Hit the cup!" The ball would get bigger and bigger against the blue sky and then fall among the tables with a thud. Then the ball would become more important than the beer. Everybody would scramble after it.

You'd have to have relief like that to hold your interest. Underneath the beer garden they had the visiting team's bull pen. We knew guys in the bull pen could hear us from the bleachers, so we'd pick out some player's number and start cheering for him. I remember the Red Sox had a catcher named Sammy White. One night we adopted him as our all-time greatest hero.

"Over there," we said. "Who's that?"

"Sammy White," someone said.

"We want *White*! WE WANT WHITE!" The poor guy didn't know what was going on. He was in the shade under the bull pen, his arms folded on his chest, his hat pulled low over his eyes.

By the time a half-inning went by, we must have had 3,000 bleacher fans chanting. Sure enough, White unfolded his arms, looks up with a quizzical smile, and starts moving to the edge of the bench. Finally, with the cheers growing even louder, he gets off the bench, comes out in the open, puts his arms in the air and starts leading the cheers like Leonard Bernstein conducting the New York Philharmonic.

The best part was still to come. The next inning, Pinky Higgins, the Red Sox manager, puts White in the game to catch. We figured we were responsible. White runs out of the bull pen, across the outfield, past the foul line, into the dugout, and puts on the shin guards. "Ladies and gentlemen," the p.a. announcer goes, "now catching for the Red Sox, number twenty-two—Sammy White!" The roar could be heard all the way to Capitol Hill.

Speaking of Griffith Stadium, I'll never forget a game one night in the summer of 1956. In fact, President Eisenhower also happened to pick that particular night to go to the game—he would frequently go unannounced to a game. Anyway, the Yankees are in town and Whitey Ford is pitching for New York.

Bottom of the second, Jim Lemon. BOOM! Home run into the beer garden. Bottom of the fourth, Lemon again. BOOM! This time, home run *over* the beer garden and into the bleachers—a 400-foot shot. Bottom of the sixth, Ford facing Lemon again. And again, BOOM!, another home run, in the exact same place as the second one, and so help me, the same guy who caught the second home run in the stands caught the third one.

Three home runs in three times at bat versus Whitey Ford.

Well, in the last of the eighth, here comes Lemon up again. STANDING OVATION. This time, however, Ford is gone and Lemon is facing Tom Morgan. Can Lemon tie the record and hit four home runs in one game? NO! Lemon fans on three pitches.

But you know what? He received another standing ovation after striking out. Could have been the only time in history that a batter struck out in a home game and received a standing ovation.

By the way, the Senators lost as usual, 6–4.

When the baseball season ended, we would keep going out on Sundays for Redskins games. Although the Redskins were losers—except for the 1955 season—they had some pretty good ball players. In 1957, for example, there was 5-foot-6-inch Eddie LeBaron at quarterback—the "Little General," as they called him. He was great. He was too small to see over the linesmen's heads, so he threw in between the lanes. That same year the Redskins came up with the "Lollipop Backfield," made up of all rookies. Ed Podoley of Central Michigan, Ed Sutton of North Carolina, and Don Bossler of Miami. However, the problem was George Preston Marshall's segregation policy.

For years Marshall, then owner of the Redskins, did not have a black player on his team. The Red Sox, the last holdout in baseball, opened the door to black players when Pumpsie Green joined them in 1959. But Marshall? Forget it. He did not integrate the club until 1962, when he acquired Bobby Mitchell from the Cleveland Browns.

Mitchell and Jimmy Brown used to tear the Redskins up when they came into town. I wouldn't be surprised if in their minds they pictured Marshall in a Redskin jersey every time they took the field.

One of the most memorable football games I saw in Griffith Stadium involved Bobby Mitchell on the field and Marshall in the owner's box. The date was November 15, 1959.

In the first quarter, the Browns give the ball to Mitchell and he goes 45 yards to the Redskins' 10. But hold everything! Marshall phones down to Joe Kuharich and the Redskins on the sidelines to ask the refs to inspect Mitchell's cleats.

Sure enough, the refs go over to Mitchell and say, "Lift up your shoes!'' They look at the cleats and start blowing their whistles. Mitchell is wearing aluminum cleats, which have not been officially approved by the league yet. The run is nullified and Mitchell, with a pair of pliers while sitting on the bench, has to replace every aluminum cleat with a rubber cleat.

The move rattles Mitchell, right? Wrong! In the second quarter, with rubber cleats on, Mitchell runs 90 yards for a touchdown, gains 232 yards on the day—which at the time was only 5 yards off Jim Brown's record—and the Browns beat the Redskins, 31–17. Funny thing is, Paul Brown took Mitchell out with one minute to go in the third quarter, and never put him back in, even though he was so close to Brown's record.

So these were my training grounds—radio and Griffith Stadium. Everything I did was either broadcasting or sports-related.

In school, forget it, nothing came easy, I always had to study to make it. But the Lord blessed me with one thing—a capacity to remember names and dates. History came easy. I could remember the generals and where they lost. I could see Pickett's charge at Gettysburg and Lee surrendering to Grant at Appomattox. I had to go to summer school twice for other subjects—algebra in high school, accounting and English literature in college—but history, no problem. I think a lot of that went back to the sports magazines. I would read that stuff and it went straight into my memory. Just like the sports stories, history had names, faces, places, things I could see.

I have a theory about reading sports that relates to women. People say, how come there aren't a lot of women sportscasters? Hey, wrong question. What you really have to ask is how come there aren't more *qualified* sportscasters, men or women? The answer is, if you haven't followed sports and read about it since you were 8 years old, there is no way in the world you can catch up. You could read from now to doomsday and you'd still be behind. You say, well, what's wrong with that? Come on, everything's wrong. There are too many smart fans out there who did read since they were 8 years old. You can't expect to stay on the air and do the job if you don't know what happened before 1940. I don't care what you know about 1970, 1980. If you don't know what happened in the 1930s, 1940s, or 1950s, no good. There are too many people out there who do know, and they'll kill you. You have to know as much, or more, than the fans. If you don't know your sports history, sooner or later they'll tune you out and watch somebody who does. It would be similar to a highschool American History teacher trying to teach school, and not knowing what happened before the First World War. No good.

What I'm saying is this: To be a sportscaster, you have to know what happened in sports before you came aboard. Otherwise, the fans will find you out.

If I knew by the age of 6 or 7 that I was going to be in radio, I was certain by the age of 14 that I was going to be a sportscaster. I had listened to Arch McDonald, Bill Stern. I could feel my voice coming down until it was full and deep. I even started to talk to an imaginary microphone like it was a person. My face would light up when I was talking. I would make gestures to the mike. When there were games at Coolidge High School in Washington, D.C., I would go behind the backstop and make believe I was doing the play-by-play. Coolidge versus Roosevelt. As far as I was concerned, it was the Yankees and the Dodgers in the World Series.

Eventually, I started my own sports show at Coolidge. They would put it over the public address system, and it would go right into the classrooms on Friday mornings. It was my first show, so to speak. ''This Day in Sports, with Warner Wolf.'' I'd give the major league ball scores from the night before, or I'd promote the upcoming football game against Wilson High. This was great. It was what I wanted to do. Come on, who wanted biology lab? Give me the scores. How many points did George Mikan score against the Celtics last night? Who would the Senators get if they traded Mickey Vernon back to Cleveland? The show also taught me how to go with a certain routine. I used to have a slogan. At the end of every sportscast, I'd say: ''This is Warner Wolf, reminding you to meet your date under the lamp post, not around it.'' Back then, I thought this was clever. It was my way of saying, ''Drive carefully.''

In college at American University, it was the same thing as in high school—a sports radio show Tuesday nights, 7:15–7:30 p.m. Even when I was a camp counselor in Darlington, Maryland, I went to ball games on my day off. The camp was located near the Maryland–Pennsylvania line. You could go to Baltimore or Philadelphia in a few hours. Going to Connie Mack Stadium, which used to be Shibe Park when the Athletics and Phillies played there, was like meeting an old friend. I had never seen it before, but I knew what it looked like because Arch McDonald used to re-create Senators-Athletics games from there. The right field wall was like a huge louvered board. It had slats in it from top to bottom. I saw Roberto Clemente hit a three-run triple off the left field wall to beat Robin Roberts. They tore Connie Mack Stadium down, just like they did Griffith Stadium. What a shame.

One of the odd jobs I had before my broadcasting career began was in a shoe store. I worked at a place at 11th and F streets, N.W., six blocks from the White House. I was an extra on Thursday nights and all day Saturday. If you were good and dedicated, you could make out well. We sold good shoes—$10 to $20 models. The way it worked is you got a percentage of everything. You sold polish? OK, you got a nickel on every quarter. You sold handbags? OK, 10 percent. The only thing was they taught you to bend the truth a little.

We'd put a pair of shoes on a lady and she'd say they were too tight. She needed a 7 instead of a 6. The problem was we didn't have any 7s. "OK, ma'am, you just wait here, we'll go get another pair," we'd say. Then we'd go in the back. They had a special machine, a kind of vice that you'd stick in the shoe and twist a few notches. It was incredible. All of a sudden you had yourself a 7. You'd put the shoe back in the box, wrap it up with new tissue paper, and rush back out. "Here we are, ma'am, see if these are a little better." They usually were.

Then I worked as an usher in the old Plaza Theater at New York Avenue and 14th Street. I never saw a theater that played the same movie for so long. *Citizen Kane, La Strada*—by the time they had completed their runs, you had the dialogue down pat.

One night there was a full house—for a sex-oriented picture—

and they showed some fish picture first, a short subject. Something to kill time with. Within minutes everybody in the theater started clapping in unison. Enough of the fish, they wanted the main feature to come on. The manager, who let me listen to Senators games on my car radio just outside the theater, kept a disciplined house. There must have been 500 people down there clapping. Too much noise. Bad for business. "Warner," he says, "go down there and tell 'em to be quiet." I was the only usher on duty. So, trying to act nonchalant, I strolled down the aisle with my flashlight at my side. CLAP! CLAP! CLAP! CLAP! They were starting to stomp their feet now, for emphasis. Finally I reached the front, turned around, and beamed the flashlight over the crowd. Never said a word. Just gave them the old flashlight beam. You know what they did? They booed me. "Get outta here!" they yelled. "Boo! Let's have the picture." "Take that flashlight and stick it up your nose!"

Another time I was standing in the rear with the manager when some guy runs back and says the woman next to him is gagging. We hurry down and find a middle-aged lady in a heavy coat choking on a hard candy. The manager tilts her over, takes his fist and smashes her right in the middle of the back. I mean, he really lets her have it between the shoulder blades. As soon as he slugs her, BOOM! the hard candy flies out. She regains her color. She begins breathing again. She looks straight into the face of the manager, who has just saved her life, and says, "Hey! Why did ya' have to hit me so hard?"

Then there was the army. Upon graduation from American University, I enlisted in the Army Reserves. I was a medic. It was the first time I'd been outside of Maryland, D.C., and Virginia except for a fraternity convention in Rochester, New York, and going to see the Phillies play in Philadelphia. I think the army is great for everyone—you learn discipline and you are humbled fast.

I spent my active duty at Fort Knox, Kentucky, and Fort Sam Houston, San Antonio, Texas. We were lined up in the barracks one day getting new fatigue shirts, the dark green ones with your name on the big white strip over the breast pocket. They gave me my shirt. "W–O–L–F," it said in big capital letters. I unfolded it and found that the sleeves were about five inches too long. Also the chest was about four sizes too large. No way I was going to wear that thing and look like a midget.

"Uh, sergeant, uh—this shirt is a little too big."

I still can remember the guy's name—Sgt. Lazana. "Tough," he says, "it's your shirt."

"Uh, sergeant, you don't understand. The sleeves . . ."

"I understand very well. You're wearing that shirt."

"Look, sergeant, I can't wear something that . . ."

He cuts me off and starts shouting. "Wolf, that's your shirt! That's the shirt I gave you, that's the shirt you'll wear!"

I'm still in civilian logic. "Uh, yes, sergeant, but you can see the sleeves. How about if I take a smaller one?"

End of conversation. Sgt. Lazana points his finger in front of the bridge of my nose.

"Wolf! You will wash the sergeant's floor. If I hear another word out of you, you will also do the latrines."

Sgt. Lazana did not hear another word out of me. I was 23 years old, and I had finally learned the real meaning of being humbled. That's the point of army discipline. You learn to swallow your pride.

I'm nobody to judge, but, in my opinion, I feel the army would have been great for a guy like John McEnroe. He'd have learned humility, discipline, and he would have learned to respect authority. There's nothing wrong with challenging authority, as McEnroe does. But there's a right way, doing it with respect for others, and a wrong way, showing no regard for your fellow man and embarrassing him in public, as he frequently does to the officials.

After four months in Texas, I came back to Washington. It was February 1961. The Redskins had finished the season 1–9–2. The old Senators were leaving for Minnesota and a new expansion team was being formed. Griffith Stadium had one more year to live. The Kennedys were new to the White House.

I began to make the rounds of the stations, looking for a job. Just give me a chance to be on. I'd have interviews but nobody seemed to want me. Finally I went to see Jim Simpson, the most respected sportscaster in town. He later went to NBC Sports and ESPN, the all-sports cable network. Back then he was with WRC radio and television.

This was the first time we met. He probably had kids coming to him for advice every week, but what he said sounded fresh. The other radio guys all gave the same advice, "You gotta go to a small-town station and get experience." That's true—you shouldn't start in a big market because there's no way you're ready—but I didn't want to hear that again. So Simpson came up with something that has stayed with me for twenty-two years.

He said, "Warner, I'm going to give you my advice. No matter what, always write your own material. Never make the mistake of reading somebody else's material. Because it'll sound like that's what you're doing." I've never read anybody else's material, but if I did I think I would feel phony. It wouldn't be me. I'd be faking it reading somebody else's material.

After Simpson gave me this lesson, I took notes and began to read from them while on the air. This forces you to fill in with your own language. You sound like you're talking to people. It's spontaneous.

There was another lesson I learned from Simpson, although he didn't bring it up that afternoon. Growing up in Washington, I noticed he always smiled at the end of his sportscast. My father used to say, "See? That's nice. He leaves his viewers with a nice feeling."

I began to practice smiling at the end of my show while still on the radio. "This is Warner Wolf," I'd say, and I'd smile. I already was performing before the mike as though it were a camera. In the back of my mind, I was in training. Hey, show the people you're enjoying yourself. You've got to smile. People have enough gloom and doom. They want to feel comfortable.

4

"There Are No Matinees"

Hearing professional sportscasters tell me I should go down to the sticks to learn the business was one thing. Hearing my father tell me was another. He could have given me advice on how to spell my name and I would have listened. ''Mensch,'' he said one day, ''I'm going to show you a story that proves there's no substitute for experience.'' So he gives me that clipping about the guy who spent fifteen years in radio and TV before getting to New York. At that moment, I knew I was headed for the bushes.

He says, ''Mensch, you gotta knock on them doors, nothin' comes easy. There are no matinees, only evening performances.'' See, he was comparing radio to the old vaudeville days. During matinees, there would be fewer people in the audience, so the performers would have a tendency to slacken off.

You know those box ads you see in the back of trade magazines? When I returned from the service, my father had me cut some tapes, and Larry Tashoff, the owner of *Broadcasting* magazine, was nice enough to help me write an ad and put it in his magazine. It said, ''College grad, military obligation fulfilled, single, money no object, willing to go anywhere.'' I got letters from Wilmington, North Carolina; Terre Haute, Indiana; a place called Miami, Oklahoma; and a guy in Pikeville, Kentucky, who also called.

''Son,'' he says, ''I've got just two questions: Do you drink, and have you ever been in jail?''

''Well, I've never been in jail,'' I say, ''and except for a beer now and then, I don't drink.''

''Hired!'' he says. ''Drive down here and I'll teach you everything there is to know.''

You want to hear a surprise? The guy was true to his word. His name was Roy Alexander. He was a short little guy with a crew cut. He paid me $40 a week, but looking back now, I probably should have paid him. The guy let me on his air even though I was no good. It was a 5,000-watt ''daytimer'' called *WLSI*, ''Radio Voice of the Big Sandy River.'' It came on the air at sunrise and went off at sundown. In summertime, we stayed on till 8 o'clock; in wintertime, 5 o'clock.

I will always be indebted to Roy Alexander because he meant what he said. I pushed the wrong buttons, missed my cues, ran the wrong commercials by mistake. Hey, I was as green as any announcer you have heard. Once a religious musical group was in the next studio recording a show to be played the next day. The theme song was ''Onward Christian Soldiers.'' Meanwhile, on the air at that moment, I was playing ''Blueberry Hill'' by Fats Domino. Somehow I pushed the wrong button and Fats Domino became the theme song for the religious show and ''Onward Christian Soldiers'' made the Top 40. Immediately Mr. Alexander came into the control room and explained where I went wrong.

Anyway, he had me do everything. News, weather, sports, music, and obituary shows. The obituary show came on every Saturday morning and was sponsored by a funeral home. It was big because the town was only 5,000 people and everybody knew everyone else.

Pikeville is in the eastern mountains of Kentucky, tucked in against Virginia and West Virginia. Since Pike County was a dry county we had to drive over the Kentucky line to Grundy, Virginia, to get a beer. I did have a membership card for the ''Green Door,'' a type of private drinking club, but I never took advantage of it.

When I first arrived in Pikeville I stayed in a white frame house owned by an elderly lady. I had the second-floor room at the back. After eating donuts every morning for two weeks before leaving for work, one morning I smelled bacon and eggs being cooked in the kitchen. It was the landlady making me breakfast, right? Wrong! It was the woman's son and two friends home from college on the weekend. Did they offer me any bacon and eggs? No! Not only that, but they were eating *my* donuts. Boo!

I moved out of there after three weeks into a place of my own. It was an apartment right on the Big Sandy River. You had your own kitchen and bath. I watched the Cincinnati Reds games, which were televised throughout Kentucky, and it happened to be a great year because the Reds won the NL pennant. But you could hear something clawing in the walls every night. Like clockwork. What was it? Rats, in the walls. Unbelievable. You'd try to go to sleep and you'd hear the rats clawing and gnawing. I told the landlord about it, and the next day he showed up with a white powder that he sprinkled just outside the apartment door.

"What's this white stuff gonna do?" I asked.

He seemed excited over the chance of fighting the rats. "Well," he said cheerfully, "they'll come out of the walls, they'll eat the white powder and it'll make their mouths burn. Then they'll go runnin' for the river, drink all the water and drown."

The guy knew his powder. BOOM! End of rats. Right into the river. Within two days the chewing stopped.

I had been on the air a few days when Mr. Alexander took me aside. "Son," he said, "there ain't nobody in Pikeville named Warner, so that ain't gonna work. You got to have a simple name. Come back tomorrow and give me a couple names."

"I've been Warner all my life," I protested.

"Nah, let's go with something simple," he said.

The next day I came back at him with Jay.

"You mean 'Jay' or the letter 'J'?" he said.

"Jay, like Joey Jay, the Reds pitcher."

"Nah, how will they know it's not the letter?" he said.

"All right, how about Robin?"

"Nah, that's a bird, man. Besides, it sounds like a girl's name."

"You mean you never heard of Robin Roberts?"

"Nah," he said. I could tell the guy wasn't a baseball fan.

"Okay," I said, "what do you think of Ken?"

"Yeah. That's it. Ken Wolf. You're Ken Wolf."

So for a half a year that's who I was. Above all else, Roy Alexander was a practical-minded man. He was the kind of guy who wanted names that people could relate to. He also meant to fulfill his obligations to the people no matter what the cost.

Once I went on the air with one of Elvis Presley's songs, "Jailhouse Rock." I had heard an old Washington disc jockey named Milton Q. Ford try this once, so I said if anybody can name this song they'll get a free bag of air. I figured "Jailhouse Rock" was an easy song, so all it would take would be a few bars of music and the station would be flooded with calls.

BOOM! No sooner had Elvis gotten through the first verse than this girl comes out of the office like a shot. She has this terribly high voice and she's scared. "Holy Moses," she says, "how are we ever gonna give 'em the gifts? All these phone calls, they're calling in every second!"

The girl was near tears. Now Mr. Alexander comes in. He was out back mowing the lawn when he heard what I had done.

"You just can't give away prizes like that," he says.

"Air," I say. "That's all. Air. The prize is air."

"Well," he says, "it's still a prize. They're gonna come in here asking for bags of air and we're gonna have to deliver." I had to go back on the radio and say that we'd run out of free bags. "That's it," I said. "Contest is over."

One of the hardest things I ever had to do was leave Roy Alexander. I hadn't promised I would stay forever, but he had treated me well. When I went in to see him, I was a little nervous. It was the first time in my life I had to tell a guy I was leaving. I was accepting a new radio position in Martinsburg, West Virginia.

"Geez," he said, the sadness showing, "you're only here six months, I taught you the business, and now that you're getting good you want to leave. You're my new guy. It isn't right."

I tried to explain that it was nothing against him. "Mr. Alexander," I said, "everything you say is true. But unless you're from

Pikeville or unless you're married, it's hard down here. People are nice and all, but there's not too much for a single guy to do.''

He didn't say anymore. I walked away and that was it.

We never talked after that but I think he may have followed my career because in 1981 he wrote me a note to see how I was doing after twenty years. He's an officer in a bank in Pikeville. ''Remember me?'' he wrote. How could I forget? I was blessed when I started out because I fell in with a guy who was honest.

I went from WLSI in Pikeville to WEPM, another small station, in Martinsburg, West Virginia. My father knew the station manager, so I had an entree. Off the air we used to call the station ''Weep 'Em'' instead of W–E–P–M. It paid only $15 more a week than Pikeville, but at least it was closer to Washington and I could drive home on weekends. Besides, they gave me back my first name.

The owner of the station was also the mayor of Martinsburg. He was not an announcer by trade, but he used to exercise his owner's rights by putting on a show from his home from midnight to 1 a.m. It was a classical music show and he had an extensive collection of records. He sat there in an armchair in his living room with the turntable at his side. He seemed to have every classical record in West Virginia—Viennese waltzes, Schubert, Mozart.

The way the show was set up was that the technician would take care of the hookup between the studio and the station owner's living room. All I would do was introduce him when I came back from commercial at the stroke of midnight.

His theme was ''Liebestraum.'' I'd start playing the theme in the background and then go into my introduction: ''And now, ladies and gentlemen, it's time for 'Midnight Classics.' '' Then he'd come on and say, ''Goooood eve–a–ning,'' very slowly. ''Time for wonderful MU-sic. Glad you could BE here.''

Everything always worked smoothly except for one night. I start playing the theme in the background, and it's coming through loud and clear. You can hear the violins. Now I start my introduction: ''Now, ladies and gentlemen, it's time for 'Midnight Classics' . . .'' But he doesn't take the cue. There's nothing but silence from the living room. I try it again: "Ladies and gentlemen, it's time for 'Midnight Classics' . . ." Still no response.

This version of "Liebestraum" is a three-minute piece, but it's already halfway done. What should I do? I'm a new guy. Should I keep playing the introduction over and over until his show is finished at 1 a.m., or should I call up to find out why he isn't on? "Come on," I'm thinking. "Get on the air."

I later found out from people at the station that on some rare occasions, the mayor had a problem staying awake for his own show. Finally, after two introductions, he came on.

Five years after I left "Weep 'Em" to go to Washington, I was invited back to town as the emcee of the Miss Martinsburg Pageant.

Now I had never been an emcee before, so I didn't know how they narrow down the field of contestants. They do it with numbers. When the judges vote to keep somebody in the running, they slip you a number which corresponds to that girl's name on your list. It's simple. You don't have to X anybody out or bother with a lot of bookkeeping. You just keep announcing the names off the numbers.

Well, I'm rolling along, cracking jokes, introducing the guest singers and comedians. I've gone through almost fifty numbers without a hitch. I remember one girl came out and danced with a dummy. When it was over I said, "Hey, all right, good show. The part of the dummy was played by the president of the Chamber of Commerce."

Finally we get to the finish. It was down to five numbers, one of which was 6 and one of which was 9. Well, you guessed it. They handed me the winning number which I thought was number 6.

I look on my list for No. 6 and see that she is Marsha Green. I look over at the finalists alongside of me. Then I say, "And the winner is—*Marsha Green!*"

It's a dream come true. Flashbulbs pop, the spotlights start whirling. The orchestra plays the Miss America melody, "Here she is, here's Miss Martinsburg . . ." Marsha's parading around, smiling. Her parents are there, she's got the crown on, they have a ramp out into the audience that is lit with tiny light bulbs. Miss Martinsburg! She's glowing, as radiant as she will ever be.

Now I look out into the audience and see the woman judge down in the orchestra pit in charge of handing me the numbers. ''No! No!'' she's yelling. She's waving her arms over her head like they do on the aircraft carriers when they don't want a plane to land. She has this frown on her face, an expression of pure pain. It was awful.

As soon as I saw her, I knew I had made a mistake. I crowned the wrong winner. She says the real winner is number 9, Sally Hollins. Do I grab the mike and say, ''Ladies and gentlemen, I made a mistake. Come back!''? Or do I let it go and have everybody find out about the real winner in the newspaper tomorrow?

I decided to tell 'em now. ''Stop the music, please, stop the music,'' I said. You could feel the air going out of the balloon. ''Ladies and gentlemen, I made a horrible mistake,'' I said. ''The real winner is Sally Hollins.''

Now here's the strange part. Instead of this terrible howling and moaning you'd expect, it was half and half. Some people actually applauded. Half of them were glad I made a mistake because they were for Sally. But the worst part of it was for the original winner. She had been parading around, holding a bouquet of roses while they played her song. I had to take her roses away, take her cape off, remove the crown from her head, and give it all to the other girl. The poor kid started crying. I apologized to her. She said, ''Oh, that's all right, that's all right.'' But it really wasn't all right. It broke her heart. I wrote the girl's family a letter apologizing, as well as the newspaper.

With the help of Bernie Harrison, a TV-radio writer at the *Washington Star* who used to know my uncle, I landed a news announcer's job at WGAY-FM in Silver Spring, Md. in late 1961. A year later I moved over to WQMR, the AM side of the station, which was big league pitching compared to Pikeville and Martinsburg. WQMR was ''Washington's Quality Music Radio.'' It was owned by a businessman, Connie B. Gay, who named the FM side after himself. At WGAY I did everything. On the hour I'd give the headlines; at quarter past, the weather; at half past, a five-minute newscast; at quarter of, the ball scores. Then you'd play the records in between. You'd run your own board, dials and all. At WQMR it was different. I was half newsman, half sportscaster—a specialist. I had my own time slot, 7:30 to 7:45 each weekday morning: "Warner Wolf and the Sports brought to you by Laurel Dodge."

Everything was great for well over a year. Then it started snowing one day in December of 1964—a bad snow—and the vice president of the station called me in the middle of a record. "Warner," he says, "they need another microphone down at the Roosevelt Hotel for the remote show we're doing tonight. I'll have somebody relieve you. Why don't you drive one down?"

"Hey, no way I'm driving down there in the snow," I said. "I've got a 1950 Ford convertible, no snow tires, it's dark out, I'm sitting in the suburbs in Silver Spring, and the Roosevelt Hotel is downtown in Washington. No way."

I don't think this went over too well. There was a pause at the other end of the line. "Uh, Warner," he said, "there's nobody else around who can bring the microphone in."

"Yeah, but haven't you seen the snow?" I argued. I knew I was being stubborn, but on the other hand I could see the stuff outside the window. Snow, sleet, and ice.

"Look, this is an order," my boss said. "I'll relieve you on the air and you go do it."

"No, *you* go do it," I said. "*You* go down there and I'll stay here."

It was almost like Sgt. Lazana and the shirt. End of conversation. The next day I was doing my show when the president of the station came in to see me. It was a big surprise; the guy was nice. "I'm sorry to have to do this," he said, "but we're letting you go. You weren't reasonable. You're not a team player. We can't have somebody working here who refuses to take orders."

Fired. I'm 26. Radio in Washington was all I ever wanted to do, and here they're telling me to get out. *Hit the road, Mack. See you later*. The strangest thing of all, though, was that I didn't feel that bad. I didn't think I had done anything wrong. I was single, I was living at home, and I had this desire to go to California anyway.

To me, California was synonymous with Hollywood. I figured

I could at least be a character actor. They had to be making a movie that needed a college kid, right? Plus my cousin Mousy was there. So was Red Skelton, who knew my folks. I bought a new 1964 Fiat for $1800 with my radio earnings and drove west.

If I thought I was happy, my actions proved otherwise. I was headed for one of the low points in my life.

As soon as I left Washington I had an obsession to keep driving. I went straight into Illinois and then cut down through the southwest.

''Keep moving, hit that pedal,'' I kept saying to myself. I breezed by St. Louis and then went from Missouri to New Mexico. It was like the Route 66 song. I'd see the cities the way the lyrics go—Joplin, Missouri; Oklahoma City; Amarillo, Texas; Gallup, New Mexico. Finally a sign said Tucumcari, New Mexico.

''Well,'' I said to myself, ''you haven't eaten anything all day, so you'd better stop.'' In my anxiety to make it to Hollywood, I had driven from six in the morning until ten that night. I finally stopped at a motel that had a small bar, a dark place decorated with sombreros and an aquarium among the liquor bottles. Unfortunately, the kitchen was closed, so instead of ordering something to eat, I ordered a beer. In fact, I had three beers—two too many on an empty stomach.

The next morning—St. Patrick's Day, March 17, 1964—I woke up in my motel bathroom with my knees on the floor and my head resting on the edge of the toilet. Totally sick. I didn't have a lot of respect for myself at that point.

Up to this time, this was the lowest I had been. I was down on myself. ''Gee,'' I said to myself, ''what's with you anyway?'' I thought my life was going nowhere. Here I'd been fired, didn't have a job, I was sick, all alone, smack in the middle of nowhere. What kind of life is this to wake up with your head on a toilet in Tucumcari, New Mexico?

I left within an hour for California. When I arrived in Los Angeles, the first thing I did was call and make an appointment with Red Skelton's secretary to see Red at the CBS studios where he was rehearsing his show. He had a TV face and a real-life face—animated on the set and expressionless off. I hung around for a few hours waiting for my chance, and I approached him when he took his first break.

"Hi, Mr. Skelton? I'm Warner Wolf. You know, Jack and Rosemary's son? They were in vaudeville with you?"

He just stared. He looked right through me as though I were a window. I could have waved my hands in front of his face and it wouldn't have helped. Finally I took out a picture of my father and mother together in the old days and showed it to him. He looked at it for a long while, then handed it back to me, got up from his seat, and went back on stage. He never uttered a word.

That night I called my father and told him the story. He said, "Well, Red always was a little strange sometimes when meeting new people."

A few weeks later Mousy, my cousin, sent me to a movie producer. This was both the beginning and the end of my career in movies.

"So you want to be in movies," he said. "What can you play?"

"You know, college kid, sports announcer, something where you need a five-foot-six guy with dark hair and a voice . . ."

He pressed a button, and when a voice answered he said, "Send in Charlie."

In walked Charlie. The guy was 6 feet, 200 pounds, muscular, looked like John Derek used to look in the 1950s. He stood there in the middle of the room, feet apart, looking down at me.

"Now here's Charlie," the producer said. "Look at him. Big, handsome, talented kid and he can't even get a part. And he's had acting training. Now look at you. You come in here off the street, and you want a part. If I hired you, what would Charlie here think?"

It was a great lesson the producer was teaching me. I was being politely humiliated. I guess Charlie was the producer's resident discourager, but he was a good one. Within the month I was back in Washington, having destroyed the engine of my Fiat on the drive back to Washington. But I had learned a few things about myself, one of which was that I was no movie star.

Two weeks after I got home my father and I were strolling

through the Wheaton, Maryland, plaza shopping center when who should we meet but the ex-boss who fired me.

"Hey, how ya' doin'?" the guy goes. We make small talk for a while, and it slowly dawns on me that the slate has been wiped clean. *It's as though nothing ever happened.* "Warner," he says, "how about coming back for us?" Not only that, but he asks me if I would be willing to take a $25 raise to $125 a week. We had a deal—and no microphones in the snow.

One other reason I came back from California to Washington, D.C., was that WMAL–Channel 7 was holding newscaster auditions. They put you before a camera and give you some copy to read. I was bad and I knew I was bad. I had watched a guy who was already on Channel 7 and I tried to imitate his voice. Terrible mistake. You've got to be yourself. After the audition the general manager asked me what happened to my voice and I was too embarrassed to tell him what I was trying to do.

I quickly proceeded to become the number one announcer in town for failing auditions. WTOP asked me to try out in October 1964 and again the following February. Each time, zero. I would tense up, and I would try to sound like an established announcer. I had the same engineer each time, Eddie Laker, and an old friend named Frank Wilson was the news director. The two of them would look at me through the glass and shake their heads. "What's with you, Warner?" they said. "You're great at WQMR—but you come here at WTOP and you sound like a different person."

If you can avoid an audition, don't take one. I just wonder how many people have failed to get jobs not because they weren't good, but because they couldn't pass an audition. Maybe it's the pressure, I don't know, but your delivery becomes affected. If you're on the air and you don't know somebody's scrutinizing you, you're more natural.

Another rule I discovered is be employed. When you're looking for a job, it's always easier when you have one. Otherwise you're at their mercy and have to take whatever they offer. When you're not working, you're desperate. When you are working, you can always stay where you are if you don't like their offer.

Finally, in April 1965 Frank Wilson asked me to give it another shot. Maybe I had a different attitude this time because I'd been through it so many times, but whatever they heard was okay.

''Welcome!'' Wilson said, shaking my hand.

I went straight to the phone to call up my father. ''See?'' he said. ''Pikeville! Martinsburg, Silver Spring, and now Washington. That was the way to do it.''

5

Interviewing the Greats in Washington

Little did I know it, but when I signed on at WTOP Radio, I had ten years of sports interviews lying ahead of me. I'm glad all the talks didn't turn out like one of the first—a bizarre one-way chat with George Halas, owner of the Chicago Bears.

In the fall of 1965 the National Football League held a meeting at the Shoreham Hotel in Washington. I was there with my tape recorder to cover it. I was practically brand new in Washington. Across the room I spotted Halas, who even then was the grand old man of pro football. I figured he'd give me a good five minutes. Eventually I'd ask him something offbeat—about how he played six games for the Yankees, some as an RF, in 1919, the year before Babe Ruth arrived. The meeting was breaking up and he was heading for the elevator just as I approached.

"Mr. Halas? Mr. Halas? Mind if I do an interview here with you? My name is Warner Wolf. WTOP radio."

Halas seemed pleased to meet me. He shook my hand and gave me a smile. Then, just as he got in front of the elevator doors he turned and said, "Warner *Wolf*, Warner *Wolf*," as though he were saying, "So you're Warner Wolf," as if he had known my name for years.

And with that, the elevator doors opened. Halas is still shaking my hand, but now he backs up into the elevator. And he's still saying, ''Warner *Wolf*, Warner *Wolf*.'' As soon as he says my name the last time the elevator doors clamp shut and I'm standing there like the guy who has missed the bus. It was Halas's way of politely avoiding the interview and not having to say no.

Then there was the time I went to the Shoreham Hotel to interview Hawk Harrelson, who was then with the Kansas City A's. (Most of the visiting teams stayed at the Shoreham.) ''You hear about the trade?'' he says. I hadn't heard. ''Oh, yeah, it's in the works,'' he says. ''I'm gonna be traded to the Red Sox.''

''No kidding,'' I say.

''Oh, yeah, this is big. It's gonna happen.''

The next year I saw Harrelson again. ''Whatever happened to that deal?'' I said.

''Ahh,'' he replied, ''don't you know what ball players do? We make up trades. We get rumors going. We give 'em to guys like you and you announce 'em and then maybe the deal will come through.''

Another time a guy calls me up one morning at the station and says, ''Did you hear? Darrell Dess, the offensive guard of the Redskins, has been traded back to the New York Giants.''

''No kidding,'' I say. Only this time I go to the phone book and find a listing for a ''D. Dess'' in suburban Maryland.

''Hello, Darrell?''

''Yes?''

''This is Warner Wolf. WTOP. Have you been traded back to the New York Giants?''

''I'm not supposed to say.''

Terrific. I went right on the radio and was the first one in Washington to report that Dess was going back to the Giants. Later that afternoon, the Redskins made the announcement official.

I did the weekend news for WTOP for half a year. During this time I was on Wednesday–Thursday–Friday, 10 a.m. to 7 p.m.; Saturday–Sunday, 5 a.m. to 2 p.m. On Sunday I had a fifteen-minute newscast at 6 a.m. It was supposed to be ten minutes of news, four minutes of sports, and one minute of weather. Instead,

I did ten minutes of sports, four minutes news, one minute weather. I guess nobody ever heard it because I got no complaints from management.

Meanwhile, I let people around the station know that I liked sports more than news. Finally, John Hays, the president of the station, who later became ambassador to Switzerland, comes to see me. "We're going to try this new concept called 'Talk Radio,' " he says. "How about answering phone calls on the air each night and talking sports? You'll be our sportscaster and we'll raise you from $7,000 to $9,000 a year." That was it. First big break. BOOM! A show of my own plus free rein to put on what I wanted.

People would call in with stumper questions. "Who was the Tigers' pitcher when Bill Veeck sent Eddie Gaedel, the midget, up to bat?" the caller would ask.

"Bob Cain," I'd say.

Then I'd turn the tables. "Bet you can't name the catcher?"

"Bob Swift!" the caller would go, trumping me.

I'd also go out during the day and tape interviews with some star or other who was in town. One of the earliest and best talks I had was with Rocky Marciano. He spoke in this thick New England accent. He had a very high voice, and when he spoke he would take his time. He was very clear and concise and he would form each word perfectly. I interviewed him twice, the first time in 1966 when he was in town for an awards banquet and again the following year when he refereed a fight in Washington at the old Uline Arena.

Marciano told me a story that shows how tough a sport boxing is. I had seen pictures of his second fight with Ezzard Charles in September 1954—Marciano won on an eighth-round knockout—and I could see that his nose was actually split from the upper part of the nostril all the way down. The nose was hanging there, all the way open. It must have been incredibly painful, being exposed, the air getting in and all.

"Rocky," I said, "didn't you feel that? How did you ever continue?"

"After Charles opened my nose," Marciano said, "I went back to my corner. My nose was numb, but I was hurting all around it, and I couldn't see it when I tried to look down cross-eyed. All I could see was blood. I started screaming at Al Weil, my manager, 'Give me a mirror! Give me a mirror! I've got to see my nose.'

"Al says, 'Nah, Rock, it's all right, it's all right. But you'd better get out there and knock him out.'

"Al just wouldn't tell me. I kept asking for a mirror because I just had to see. I tried to touch the nose but I couldn't feel it with my gloves on. Al just said make this the round, go knock him out. That's when I knew something was awfully wrong. I went out and knocked out Ezzard in the eighth round."

You know what Rocky seemed proudest of? The fact that he was a professional ball player as well as a fighter. He was a catcher in the Chicago Cubs organization. "I couldn't hit the curve," he said, "but nobody stole on me. I'd rifle that thing down to second and they were out by ten feet. And they were afraid to come into the plate and bowl me over. I was five eleven, one eighty-four, just like I was when I fought. I'd put the tag on 'em so hard they wouldn't forget."

Marciano was only 33 when he retired. He quit on top, right in his prime, with a record of 49–0. I asked him why he didn't fight at least one more time before he retired, so he would have a record of an even 50–0.

"Well," he said in that high New England accent, "I knew it was time to stop when I disliked going to the gym. The fighting and the banging and the pain I could take. But there came a time when the training bored me. I was known as a puncher, but my whole thing was to be in better shape than my opponent. I'd wear him down before he wore me down. I'd fight the fifteenth round with as much power and stamina as I had in the first round. So I knew what lack of training would mean. I wouldn't be able to give my best and I would probably lose. Rather than lose, I got out."

At the time of our talk lots of people were calling Muhammad Ali the greatest fighter of all time. So I asked Marciano the inevitable question: "If you had both been able to fight each other in your primes, what would have happened?" His response was interesting.

"I've pictured the fight in my head many times," Marciano

said. "He would've hit me with a terrible number of punches. His jab is awfully fast [*fahst*, as Rocky pronounced it]. But I've fought others who were fast. I've fought others who were knockout punchers, whereas Ali is a TKO puncher. If he didn't cut me up—and despite the Charles fight, I'm not an awful bleeder—I think I would have eventually caught up with him in the late rounds. He wouldn't have been able to take my punch. I would have stalked him and worn him down. In the thirteenth, fourteenth, or fifteenth round he would've been mine. I would've trained well for the fight. I would've been able to endure a lot."

They say another big fight would have been Marciano against Jack Dempsey. Hey, there's no question Dempsey was great, perhaps the hardest puncher of all times. They didn't call him the Manassa Mauler for nothing. He just tore Jess Willard apart, and Willard was a six-foot-six, 245 pound giant. But except for many exhibition matches, Dempsey had only six title fights in seven years when he was champion.

After the Luis Firpo fight in September 1923, Dempsey (except for the exhibitions) did not have another fight until the first Gene Tunney fight in September 1926. That's three years apart.

Whenever Dempsey's and Tunney's names are mentioned, the famous long count of September 1927 comes to mind. It was their second fight. It was the first championship fight in Illinois in which both fighters agreed to go to a neutral corner in case of a knockdown. Before this, you could stand over your opponent and hit him the instant he got up again. When Dempsey knocked Tunney down in the seventh round, he forgot about the new knockdown rule. He just stood there over Tunney out of habit. It took between five and seven seconds for referee Dave Barry to take him to a neutral corner, and only then did the count begin. Tunney got back to his feet at the count of nine, although he really was on the canvas anywhere from fourteen to sixteen seconds. Sure enough, Tunney went on to win the fight and everybody said what a shame it was for Dempsey.

However, when I met Dempsey at the National Press Club in 1965, he made an interesting statement.

"Warner," he said, "I got more mileage and favorable publicity out of losing that fight than if I had knocked Tunney out. It's ridiculous, but I think some people loved me because they thought I was robbed."

If you put a stopwatch on the film of that fight, you'll see that Tunney is down between fourteen and sixteen seconds. The question people ask is, "Could Tunney have gotten up at the count of nine if there hadn't been a long count?" The answer is yes, because Tunney appears to be looking squarely at referee Dave Barry, watching his count, ready to get up at nine. You can see that in the films. But the *real* question is, "Would Tunney have had a clear enough head to stay away from Dempsey *after* he got up if there hadn't been a long count?" *That*'s the question.

By far the biggest surprise I ever had on radio was Ali paying a visit to my studio. You've got to realize this was 1968. Ali had refused to submit to the draft—"I got nothin' against them Viet Cong," he said, referring to the Vietnam War—and the state boxing commissions had stripped him of his title. But his reputation was still that of a bigmouth. Most people accused him of dodging the draft.

I used to know a restaurateur in Washington. One day he calls and says, "Hey, Warner, you want Ali tonight?" I couldn't believe it. Here's this guy promising to deliver the former champion to my show. Come on, who was I to have Ali on my show? "Yeah, bring him on. Absolutely," I said. It was such a big thing to have Ali that I was afraid to announce it when I went on the air at 7:30. I was afraid the guy wouldn't deliver, so I just kept taking calls.

At ten minutes to eight I look up and who do I see through the glass window of the studio but Ali and three bodyguards. They were all big guys. Without saying a word, Ali opens the studio door, walks in, pulls up a chair, and looks at me with that wide-eyed expression. "Ladies and gentlemen," I say, "*do I have a surprise for you!* Here he is, the former heavyweight champion of the world . . . MUHAMMAD ALI!"

I couldn't believe this guy. Ali talked for almost an hour to me and the people who called up. Then I realized how smart this guy was. It would be two more years before his reinstatement fight with

Jerry Quarry, and it would be three more years before he'd meet Joe Frazier. But he was already drumming up publicity for the Frazier fight. He did that poem which he's done eighty-nine times since, about Frazier being the first black satellite going into space:

> Now Ali lands with a right;
> What a beautiful swing!
> But the punch lifts Frazier
> Clear out of the ring!
>
> Frazier's still risin',
> But the referee wears a frown,
> 'Cause he can't start countin'
> Till Frazier comes down.
>
> Now Frazier disappears from view,
> The crowd is getting frantic;
> Our radar stations have picked him up;
> He's somewhere over the Atlantic.
>
> Who would've thought
> When they came to the fight
> That they would witness the launching
> of a black satellite?

Another thing which impressed me was that Ali had no notes. He did all this poetry extemporaneously—and it all came out in rhyme! He had answers for everything.

After the show I walked him out to his limo. As Ali sank into the back seat he turned and said, "This is a promise: When I get to be champ again, I'll be back."

The next time I saw Ali was in 1969 in a downtown Washington hotel. By now I was on WTOP television as well as radio. He had a computerized fight that year with Marciano in which both men got into the ring and acted out the computer's script by pulling their punches. The promoters sent the film around to the theaters and it did pretty well. Nobody knew who "won" because different endings were filmed. Anyway, I have him on my show and we're both sitting on these stools when I say, "Show me, what kind of punches did you use? How did you hit Marciano if you didn't want to hurt him?''

Ali throws this left jab at me but pulls it just in time so I hardly feel it. Playing the role to the hilt, I tumble off the stool holding my stomach. All of a sudden a look of concern comes over Ali's face. ''C'mon, get up, get up,'' he says. ''I didn't hurt you.'' After lying there for ten seconds, I begin to laugh, and he says to me, ''Hey, do you mean to tell me you were fakin'? People are gonna think I hurt you.''

The thing about Ali is there are two sides to the guy—the humorous Ali and the serious Ali. If he didn't have a fight coming up, he could be so serious and reflective you sometimes couldn't hear him. But if he had a fight to promote coming up, he was great.

One afternoon in 1970, a member of Ali's entourage calls up and says, ''We'll be there in two hours.'' It was usually sudden like that. Ali would descend upon you when you didn't expect it. Just as he promised, the limo pulls up in time for the 6 p.m. show. Out steps Ali, his bodyguards, his hangers-on. School kids suddenly appear out of nowhere. ''Geez,'' I'm thinking, ''this is like the Pied Piper.'' Before you know it, there's a mob scene as Ali moves to the front door.

We went onto the set and sat down. He was gonna put Frazier into orbit, he was gonna give everybody a bigger whuppin' than he gave Sonny Liston. He was the prettiest—he was the greatest. He was also something else: He was the greatest ticket seller of all time.

Little did I realize it, but all during the late 1960s I was learning how to interview people. It looks easy but forget it, you have to master the art. Johnny Carson has it. His secret is getting the response, letting the guest talk and listening to what the guest is saying. Notice, most of Carson's follow-up questions are in response to what the guest has just said. Carson listens. Too many people think they're good interviewers if *they* talk a lot. But it's the guest whom the people want to hear, not the interviewer. It's like umpiring. People don't go to the game to see the umpire. The less he's noticed, the better. It's the players they want to see. Same thing in broadcasting. A lot of interviewers also make the mistake of asking too long a question. By the time the guest gets a chance to answer, you've already lost the audience.

One of the people who taught me to be concise in an interview was Ted Williams, who managed the Washington Senators from 1969 to 1971. What an interview this guy was! You had to ask direct, intelligent questions or he would cut you off, you were wasting his time. But ask him something specific—"Hey, Ted, do you remember the time you went four-for-four in Philadelphia?"—and he was off to the races. The man is phenomenal. He can recall every pitch, every pitcher, every count, and where the ball went when he hit it.

However, a Ted Williams interview was over *when Ted decided it was over*. It didn't matter where you were in the interview. He'd say thank you and get up and leave. No warning. He'd had enough. This was just the way he was.

In 1969 Williams took a lousy team and yet finished in fourth place in the American League East, 86–76, just one game behind Boston. It was incredible. They all hit over their heads. They listened to Williams and thought they could hit like him. Eddie Brinkman, the shortstop, who hit .187 the year before, hits .266. First baseman Mike Epstein, a .244 lifetime hitter, hits .278, 85 runs batted in, 30 home runs. Third baseman Ken McMullen, .248 lifetime, goes .272, 19 homers, 87 RBI. Right fielder Hank Allen, .241 lifetime, hits .277. Center fielder Del Unser, who hit .230 the year before, goes .286. And Frank Howard, the left fielder—BOOM!—.296, 48 homers, 111 RBI.

So coming back from Minnesota after the last road trip, I sat down next to Williams on the plane and said, "Ted, you ought to quit right now. Except for Frank Howard you'll never get these guys to do this again in a million years. You knew how to quit after hitting a homer in your last at bat as a player. So do it again as a manager, and get out now."

Williams looked me straight in the eye and laughed. He just laughed. He liked guys who would speak their piece. If you weren't afraid of him, he thought you were all right.

Once I asked him where his career would've gone if he hadn't broken his arm in the 1950 All-Star Game. He said he might have hit .400 again, but he could never get the old snap into his swing again after the arm was broken. Amazing. The guy hit .388 in 1957 as a 39-year-old without any snap. Who knows what he would have done if he could have brought his arm around? He was the greatest pure hitter I ever saw.

By 1969 I was doing the Senators games on radio and TV. Washington had an outfielder that year who could hit a long ball but was not one of the greatest fielders of all time. One night we were in Minnesota. Harmon Killebrew of the Twins swings and hits a fly ball to medium left field. The outfielder, after coming in and going out, finally circles under the ball and makes a one-handed grab. Right after the catch I say, "He's the only outfielder in baseball who can make a routine catch seem exciting!"

Well, he didn't think my remark was so funny. Apparently somebody from Washington called him in the clubhouse right after the game. I'm getting on the bus with the Senators to go back to the hotel and he sits down beside me.

Suddenly he says, "I know what you said about me and I don't think it's funny. Furthermore, I know what's really wrong. You're out to get me because you don't like me dating your sister's girlfriend."

I turned to him and pointed out that I don't have any sisters or brothers. I'm an only child. He couldn't accept the fact that he was not a good outfielder. He had it in his mind that I was picking on him because I had something against him personally.

A few years later I was standing in a bar in Georgetown when the placekicker of the Washington Redskins turned up at my side. It just so happened that the previous week I had said on my show that the Redskins have to get a kicker who can put the ball into or out of the end zone on kickoffs because they were getting killed on field position. In those days, you kicked off from the 40, not the 35.

"Well," the kicker says, "I heard what you said on your show, but you're missing the point. You worry about hang time, not distance. We're supposed to kick 'em high, not necessarily long."

No way he could convince me of that argument. No way, man. Why let them return the kickoff to the 30 or 40? Come on, kick off into or out of the end zone and let them have it at the 20. How come all the other teams kick it long and high?

I'm happy to say that in my twenty-two years of broadcasting, these are the only two instances I know of where I've been personally challenged by athletes over something I've said on the air.

In certain respects, radio is more fun than being on television. In 1966 I set up a radio show called *Two Minutes to Go*. It was a takeoff on CBS radio's old college football roundup show in which reporters would phone in live reports from the press box during the game's last two minutes.

The audience liked the show because it was before they had NFL doubleheaders on television. In those days, radio was how you found out the scores around the league. There were no highlight shows like *The NFL Today* or *NFL '83*. All you saw was the game involving your team. And because the blackout rule was still in effect, you wouldn't have any TV at all if your team was playing at home. So borrowing the idea from the old college football show, we lined up reporters in six or eight cities who would call in to WTOP with running commentary as their game came to an end. A lot of people would listen on their car radios as they were driving home from the Redskin game around 4 o'clock.

The idea, of course, was not just to give the scores, but to make things interesting. It was the "You Are There" approach. I wanted the reporters to give the people some play-by-play. Most of the guys went along with it, making every game sound like the most dramatic in history.

There was a guy in Philadelphia named Red McCarthy. Red was a loyal Eagles fan who would really get excited during his two minutes.

In one particular game, the Cowboys trailed the Eagles 17–16 but had the ball deep in Eagles territory. There were less than two minutes to go. Don Meredith had just completed a pass for a first down, but the Cowboys needed to get a little closer to make sure of the winning field goal.

Red says, "All right, folks, Meredith breaks the huddle and

follows the Cowboys to the line. He's over his center now, barking those signals. He's looking right, looking left—there's the snap! Meredith back to pass. He throws . . .

"Aaaaaaaahhhhhh! Aaaaaaaahhhhhh!" All of a sudden Red starts screaming for joy. *"Aaaaaaaahhhhhh! Aaaaaaaahhhhhh!"* In the background the crowd is going berserk. You can hear Red pounding his fist on the table next to the microphone. It seemed like an eternity. *"Aaaaaaaahhhhhh! Aaaaaaaahhhhhh!"*

"Red, Red! Tell us what happened," I said.

Finally he calms down and picks up the microphone. "The Cowboys fumbled and the Eagles recovered. Can you believe it? It's the Eagles' ball."(The Eagles won 17–16.)

Two Minutes to Go. It was quite a show. We had to cancel it the following year, though. There was a broadcast rights problem with the NFL. No play-by-play, even for two minutes, unless we were the original station who purchased the rights to the game!

As good as those games were, no final two minutes were able to rival the climax of a game I did in April 1966—the seventh and final game of the National Basketball Association finals between the Boston Celtics and the Los Angeles Lakers. Forget all the other games I announced. This was by far the most exciting.

I knew Red Auerbach, the coach of the Celtics, because he was from Washington, D.C. So when Lloyd Dennis, the president of WTOP, tells me to do the play-by-play and arrange transmission of the potential seventh game from the Boston Garden, I give Auerbach a call. I'll never forget this. It's a week before the seventh game, if there is going to be one. The Celtics are ahead in the series, 3 games to 1, and I'm asking Red can we do the championship game if it goes to the limit. He puts the phone down and says to his secretary, "Give credentials to Warner Wolf and WTOP for the seventh game back here next Thursday." He must have had a premonition that the Lakers were going to win game five in Boston and game six in Los Angeles to send the series back to the Garden. It was such a tight series and the teams were so evenly matched that he had a sixth sense.

By the way, when speaking of Red Auerbach it must be stated

he is in a class by himself when it comes to judging talent. No one comes close when it comes to making trades. What separates Auerbach from the rest of the GMs and coaches is that Auerbach can see the overall picture and immediately recognize what particular player he needs to complete the mix. He needed a center, he got Robert Parish from Golden State. He needed a playmaker, he gets Quinn Buckner from Milwaukee. Whatever the Celtics needed, Auerbach recognized it and then went out and got it.

Oh, you know why the Celtics have always worn black shoes? Because in the early days, when the Celtics were not making any money, to cut down on costs Auerbach had the Celtics wear black shoes because you couldn't tell they were dirty, and therefore you didn't have to wash 'em as much as white shoes and could wear 'em longer.

Anyway, I'm sitting in the balcony broadcast booth in Boston as game seven begins. Now I don't mind telling you, this was a thrill. I had never done an NBA game before, much less the championship. I had done the American University and Maryland University basketball games, but this was the big leagues, and this was the hallowed Boston Garden with the title flags hanging from the rafters. What more could a guy want? I got so pumped up and was talking so loud and fast in the first half that the phone rings next to my announcing position. My engineer, a local man from Boston, picked it up, listened a moment, and hung up.

During a commercial, the guy leaned over to me. "Do you know a Lloyd Dennis?"

"Yeah. He runs the station we're doing this game for."

"Well, he says to tell you that if you don't calm down, you're not going to have a voice for the second half."

It was good advice. The final minute was frantic. Thirty seconds to go, Bill Russell takes a feed from K. C. Jones, dunks one over Leroy Ellis, and it's 95–85, Boston. The Garden is going crazy. "Well," I said, "that's it. Red Auerbach is lighting up his victory cigar."

Meanwhile, Jerry West takes the ball for the Lakers, 30-foot jump shot—SWISH!—95–87 Celtics.

As the Celtics throw the ball in, West steals it, scores again, and it's 95–89 Celtics. Fifteen seconds left and the Celtics call time out. By now thousands of fans had come down from the stands and completely surrounded the court.

After the time-out, Sam Jones accidentally dribbles the ball out of bounds. Walt Hazzard to Ellis to Jim King, who lays it up and in, 95–91 Celtics. The clock is still running. Ten seconds left. The Celtics throw it in, but Sam Jones loses the ball. West to Ellis, 20-footer, SWISH—95–93, Celtics. Five seconds left. I see Auerbach sitting next to Governor John Volpe of Massachusetts. ''Auerbach may have to put out that cigar,'' I say.

Finally, K. C. Jones throws the ball in to Larry Siegfried. Siegfried throws the ball straight up in the air. By the time the ball comes down the buzzer goes off and the Celtics are champions, 95–93. What a game to broadcast!

As far as radio interviews go, I remember one once with a punt returner for the Redskins named Ricky Harris. Harris was an excellent punt return man. I saw him rip off a 76-yarder against the Giants and another against the Eagles. My first year on the radio I threw him a question I always wanted to ask. ''Say you've caught the punt, eleven bodies are thundering down the field at you, and ten of your guys are out there trying to block 'em. What is it like at the exact instant you look up the field?''

''You know what it's like?'' he said. ''It's like a camera shutter opening and closing when you take a picture. You look for a hole. It's there and it's gone.'' He snapped his fingers. ''It's about one-tenth as fast as that. You have about that much time to figure out where you're going to go. *Click!* The shutter closes before you know it's open. And before it closes you've got to make up your mind.''

Another interview was with Vince Lombardi. Right after he signed as coach of the Redskins in 1969, he took all the media guys out to lunch at Duke Ziebert's restaurant. He had a reputation of putting fear into people—including reporters—but he could also be a charming guy. I remember he had two Bloody Marys. He said, ''I hope you gentlemen don't think I'm a drinker, but it's out of season and I will have a second Bloody Mary because I'm enjoying myself.''

That was the thing with Lombardi and a lot of other coaches. They're like Dr. Jekyll out of season and Mr. Hyde in season. I've seen it with baseball managers too. As far as aging a person goes, I've got to equate it to being president of the United States. It's the responsibility and the pressure. You know those pictures of Jimmy Carter and Richard Nixon, how they aged from year to year? I've seen it in managers and coaches. I remember Mayo Smith, who was the manager of the Detroit Tigers when I used to do the Senator games. He was one of the few managers who used to come into the press room after the game, win or lose, and have a drink with the press. Boy, did he look haggard. He was manager of the Tigers and they were going nowhere. Then he was fired and I saw him a year later. The guy looked ten years younger.

Lombardi was very outgoing and friendly in the off-season. We had a lively debate about which player threw the best halfback option pass. He said it was Frank Gifford and that he had taught him how to perfect it when he was an assistant coach with the Giants. Then he said something that caught my attention. He had coached Paul Hornung at Green Bay. "You know what made him great inside the five-yard line like no other player? *He loved the glory*. That's why he always scored a touchdown when he got that close. Give him the ball, it's a touchdown. He loved the glory like no other player I've ever coached."

I've never seen a coach or manager madder than Lombardi got on November 16, 1969, in a game with the Cowboys.

I was sitting in the upstairs sun deck at RFK Stadium, the same seats my father and I had bought years before. The Redskins were getting blown out in the first half, embarrassing Lombardi. Bob Hayes ran one back 80 yards for a touchdown. The Redskins trailed 24–7, second quarter.

But gradually the Redskins begin to stage a comeback. Sonny Jurgensen starts throwing to Charley Taylor and Jerry Smith. Early in the fourth quarter it's now 34–28 Dallas, and the Cowboys are forced to punt to Ricky Harris.

Harris gets the ball on his own 14 and comes up the sidelines. Suddenly the Redskins form a wall. They're cutting the Cowboys down one by one, giving Harris a clear road. The last block is thrown by Chris Hanburger at the Dallas 30. Cowboys are lying all over the field. Harris runs into the end zone and the stadium goes crazy, because with the extra point the Redskins will lead, 35–34. It's one of the greatest comebacks in Washington history.

But hold everything. People in the stands are pointing to a flag on the field. The last block by Hanburger is called clipping. NO TOUCHDOWN! You should have heard that stadium. The fans booed for two minutes. And Lombardi went crazy. You could see him screaming. He was so mad that Bill Austin, an assistant coach, put a bear hug on him to hold him back. He actually wanted to run out on the field at the referee. The Redskins ultimately lost, 41–28, but Lombardi is what I remember.

Funny, but I never interviewed Lombardi other than at that luncheon. I once tried to talk to him when he was coaching the Packers in the mid-1960s. When the Packers came east to play the Colts they would train for the week at the Washingtonian Motel in Gaithersburg, Maryland, a suburb of Washington. I went to see him and he gave me The Look. "Wow, what a scowl," I said to myself. "Stay away from this guy. I don't think he wants to be interviewed." I taped something with Don Chandler instead. Man, was that a tough look Lombardi had.

I never claim to be a journalist—as I've been saying, I'm a sports commentator, an entertainer—but I was fortunate enough to break the story of Lombardi's move to Washington. I predicted he would coach the Redskins several months before it was announced. It's the only major story in my twenty-two-year career that I can honestly say I had before anybody else in the *country*.

Lombardi had retired from coaching and was general manager of the Packers in 1968. Early in 1969 I went on the air at Channel 9 and said, "Lombardi will be the next coach of the Redskins." Simple as that, "coach of the Redskins." People thought I was nuts. I didn't have much of a following on TV yet—I had begun only a few weeks before—so everybody ignored it. But one newspaperman called me up. Tom Yorke of the old Washington *Daily News* phoned me at home and said, "What is this? How can you predict such a thing?"

I gave him the rundown. First, I knew that Edward Bennett Williams, the president of the Redskins, had had dinner with Lombardi in New York. Second, I knew a real estate agent who had shown a house in Potomac, Maryland, to someone representing Lombardi. Third, I had read Lombardi wasn't happy being a general manager and wanted to get back into coaching. Fourth—this was the clincher—I knew a bellhop at the Mayflower Hotel in Washington who said he had just seen Lombardi check out after a very quiet visit to town. I figured, how sure can you be? This was common sense. So I went with the prediction on the air. The newspapers didn't print it for two more months.

To me, the human side of Lombardi re-emerged after the 1969 season. The Redskins finished 7–5–2, which was their first winning season since Joe Kuharich had them in 1955. I never talked to Lombardi during the season. He really didn't go for this interview stuff. He'd send Austin to represent him. But the following spring I'm standing in the press room of RFK for the opening game of the baseball season and there's Lombardi. I saw him out of the corner of my eye. Now remember, he's not a guy you walk up to. It was just with my peripheral vision that I saw him.

What happened next was one of the biggest thrills of my life at that time.

"Hey, Warner!" Lombardi says. "Come on over here." He was asking *me* to go over *there*. He was resting on a wooden chair. "Sit down," he says. "Warner, I thought I'd tell you that I enjoy your work on television. I think you're fair, and that's the most important thing."

I didn't know what to say. He called me over to tell me I'm fair. Wow! Only later that year did I learn that Lombardi was dying of cancer. He had intestinal cancer, just like my father did four years before.

It was the last time I saw him. I remember he stayed in the chair a long time, just observing people go by. He died at Georgetown Hospital a few months later.

6

You Gotta Have Someone in Your Corner

Let me tell you something about television. You can have the greatest voice in the world, you can be the funniest guy at the station, and the people in their homes can love you. But if you don't have a good management person in your corner, forget it, it's all over. Television is different from radio. The stakes are higher. If some sponsor or rights holder doesn't like you and your station doesn't back you up, that's it. Off the air. Find another line of work.

I started doing television shows—games, interviews, sportscasts—for WTOP–Channel 9 in 1969. It was weird. Within months after I came over from the radio side there were people who wanted me off the air. "No good. Get rid of this guy," they'd say. They didn't like what I was saying.

One of the first people I had a problem with was the late Bob Short, a trucking magnate from Minnesota who had bought the Washington Senators. Short was a political operator in the Democratic party, well connected in Washington. He was used to getting his way. We had our differences because I criticized the Senators. Even Ted Williams, the manager, criticized them in public, so how could they complain about me? They were a bad, bad team except for that one year in 1969 when Williams had them playing over their heads.

Anyway, there was one game between the Senators and the Orioles in 1970 that did not exactly endear me to Short. The Senators were on their way to one of their customary last-place finishes while the Orioles were headed for a second straight pennant. The game was in Washington, a 1–1 tie, top of the ninth. Baltimore gets a couple men on, they execute a perfect sacrifice bunt, and Mark Belanger knocks in the go-ahead run with a grounder to second. In the bottom of the ninth the Senators get the first man on base, but the next guy strikes out trying to bunt, and the next batter grounds into a double play. Game's over. Terrible! Boo! "Ladies and gentlemen," I said in my recap after the game, "there's the difference between a first-place club and a last-place club. One can bunt and the other can't. There's your difference in this ball game and there's your difference in the teams."

I was told that Short hit the roof. He listened to all the games, sometimes via a phone hookup in Minnesota. No way am I going to criticize his Senators. Larry Israel, the chairman of WTOP, tells me Short called him and said, "Get Wolf off! I've spent a lot of money on your station. I gave the games to you. I don't want this criticism."

Israel told me he told Short that he picks his own announcers. Israel said as long as I'm here, Warner Wolf is going to do the games.

See what I mean? You have to have somebody in your corner. If you don't you're dead. Somebody other than Israel might have taken me off the games.

In 1970 Short raised ticket prices, cutting out bargains for clergymen, firemen, and policemen unless they wore their uniforms to the park, and also scheduled two exhibition games in Dallas in 1971. And after the 1970 season was over, he traded the shortstop, Eddie Brinkman, and the third baseman, Aurelio Rodriguez, to Detroit for Denny McLain and three others. The whole left side of the infield was gone. To me, it was obvious what was happening. This guy was going to move the club.

"Nah, nah," Short says, "I'm not going anywhere."

I come on the air and say, "The signs point to a move. It's so long, Senators. If I'm wrong, give me a boo, but I'm telling you, this guy is gonna move the club."

Israel told me Short called him up again and said, "C'mon, what is this stuff? I'm not going anywhere. Get Wolf off the air. He has no right to come on and say that I'm moving the club."

Of course you know what happened. At the end of 1971, Short moved the club to Arlington, Texas, where they've been ever since.

Then there was a TV director behind the scenes at Channel 9 who almost succeeded in knocking me off the Redskins' exhibition games in 1969. When the station got the rights to the games, I had a shot at doing the color commentary.

Channel 9's program director calls me in. "Warner," he says, "you're not going to do the games. We understand the Redskins don't like you because you knock 'em."

"Who says that?"

"The director."

"The director's wrong. It isn't true."

"Well, that's what *you* say. This is our decision."

I couldn't believe it—man, was *that* unfair!

Now this is the only time I've done this. I call up Edward Bennett Williams, president of the Redskins, who had always been very nice to me. I say, "Mr. Williams, I was told that the Redskins don't like me and that's why I'm not going to do the color commentary."

"Who told you that?" he says.

"The program director."

"Tell me this, Warner: Do you want to do the Redskin games?"

"Yessir."

"Consider it done," he says. BOOM! Just like that. *"Consider it done!"*

Next day the program director calls me in again. "Uh, Warner," he says, "we've changed our minds on those games. We got this call from Edward Bennett Williams. He wants you to do the games."

Sometimes you have to go over the boss's head. It had to be done.

During those early years at Channel 9, I developed a lot of sayings. Stuff like the "Boo of the Week," "Hey, Gimme a Break!"

"BOOM!" and "SWISH!" Most of the expressions just came naturally. But the "Boo of the Week" I owe to a lawyer and friend of mine in Washington named Dick Beyda. Instead of saying, "That's bad," he'd say, "That's a boo, man, that's a boo." Nothing special. Just a way of talking. So when I went on the air, I said, "How about a Boo of the Week!" People started looking for it and it became successful.

One of my early Boos of the Week was on Thanksgiving Eve, 1970. The Redskins cut a center named John Didion. I went on the air at 6 o'clock. "To cut Didion on Thanksgiving Eve is one of the cruelest moves I've seen," I said. "Come on, at least why not wait until after Thanksgiving? It's heartless to cut a man on the eve of Thanksgiving. Besides, it's like saying Didion is the scapegoat for the Redskins' poor season."

BOO Redskins, I said at the end of the show. That night, Bill Austin, the coach of the Redskins, came in to tape his weekly TV show. Before we begin to tape, he really chews me out for criticizing the Redskins. I told him if he didn't like what I said, he should change his TV dial. We got along fine after that.

Another early boo I gave involved the Clay Kirby game in 1970. Clay Kirby was a pitcher for the San Diego Padres who in the off-season lived in Arlington, Virginia, just across the river from Washington. Nice angle: Local boy makes good. He has a no-hitter going in the ninth inning against the Mets when his manager, Preston Gomez, takes him out. Unbelievable! Scoreless tie, the kid puts two guys on base with walks in the ninth, and the manager takes him out, even though Kirby has a no-hitter going.

Afterward, everybody asks Gomez how he could be so heartless to take Kirby out. "It's my job to try to win every game," he says. "Personal records don't come first."

Boo, man, *boo!* This is August and the Padres are twenty-six games out of first. No way on earth the game means anything other than the no-hitter. I go on the air and give Gomez the Boo of the Week.

Now the nice thing about Gomez is he knew the difference between a boo, which is entertainment, and me not liking him. I'd see him in one city or another where he was later a third-base coach, and he was always friendly. I'd shake his hand, he'd shake mine.

Actually, the boo is half serious, half in jest. There's never any malice. It's just like booing at the ball park. I remember booing Calvin Griffith once in 1962 after he had moved the original Senators to Minnesota. Me and my buddies were in our mid-twenties. It was right after a Senators–Twins game at Kennedy Stadium. We saw Calvin standing near an exit of the ball park, and we drove by and booed him. You know how kids moon guys today? Well, we just booed then.

Many times later while on the air, I booed Calvin because of his famous statement in January 1958 in the *Washington Post*, that the Senators would remain in Washington forever. Upon the conclusion of the 1960 season, Griffith moved the Senators to Minnesota.

Don't get me wrong. It bothered me, what he did. But when you boo, it's never meant to be personal. Ironically, I would do Senators' games from Minnesota later on, and there he was in the press room. I couldn't really be mad at him. He would invite me over to sit down. I guess he had friends in Washington who would tell him I was tough on him. I think he always felt a little bad about moving.

My saying "SWISH!" came from an expression we used to use on the playgrounds. When a guy took a shot and it went clean through the basket, we'd all say, "SWISH!" No rim, no backboard, just clean through. SWISH! So, when I came on TV and narrated basketball highlights, it was a natural.

Same thing with "BOOM!" We'd be playing softball—I used to play a lot of softball when I was a kid. A guy would hit a ball and the whole team would go, "BOOM! Good shot! BOOM! There it goes! BOOM!" On the highlights, I figured, hey, why not? BOOM! Let the people hear it.

People often ask, "Where did 'Gimme a Break!' and 'Let's Go to the Videotape!' come from?"

Well, "Gimme a Break!" originated from a sportscast I did at WTOP in Washington. I was showing highlights of a Redskin game.

There was an interference call that could have gone either way, but it went against the Skins. I said, "Come on, ref, give me a break!" The cameramen and the people on the set began to laugh. So the next night, I used it again in another instance. *"Gimme a break!"* Same response in the studio. I've used it ever since.

As far as "Let's Go to the Videotape"—that serves a different purpose.

One night, also at WTOP, I was getting ready to show the tape of a Lakers–Warriors game. I say, "OK, let's look at Kareem Abdul-Jabbar versus Nate Thurmond last night."

No tape.

Again I say, "OK, let's look at Jabbar last night."

No tape.

Finally, I say to the director, Ernie Baur, "Hey, Ernie, roll the Jabbar tape!"

Still, *no tape.*

Finally, out of desperation, I said, *"OK, let's go to the videotape!"* With that, the tape comes on. Thus, "Let's Go to the Videotape!" was born.

The reason it works is this: You must realize, a director in the control room has ten things to do at once. He's constantly busy and oftentimes will miss the roll cue for the videotape. However, a director can be doing 10 million other things, but once he hears those magic words—*"Let's go to the videotape!"*—he will put everything aside and roll that tape. It's like a reflex action. When a director hears *"Let's go to the videotape!"* he rolls it.

During my eleven years in Washington as a broadcaster, I was twice invited to the White House. The first time was 1969 when Richard Nixon had the baseball players and the press over for the All-Star Game, which was in Washington. One announcer from each local station was invited. The second time was 1974 when Gerald Ford invited me and my wife to a White House dinner. "Why me?" I kept saying. It turned out Ford was a big sports fan and watched me on the local news in Washington. We got through the gates because we had a pass, but as we approached the circular driveway in the back of the White House, four Secret Service guys came out asking who I was. I think the fact that we had a little Toyota, coming in with all those other limos, made 'em suspicious.

One of the funniest things that happened to me on television had nothing to do with sports. In 1969 Larry Israel thought I was popular enough to do an afternoon personality show for women. Four-thirty to 5 o'clock, one-half hour—movie stars, writers, politicians. The show died in six months. But it was a good experience. We had all kinds of different guests, including the late Jack E. Leonard, the comedian. Wow, was this guy something!

My wife and I saw him the evening before at the Cellar Door, a nightclub in Georgetown. After he does his show I go backstage and ask him if he will come on my TV show. "Yeah," he says, "but only if you pick me up. Gotta pick me up and bring me back. I don't drive and I don't take taxis."

The next day I show up at his hotel, the Key Bridge Marriott, just across the Potomac River from Washington. It's about a fifteen-minute drive from the television station—too long for Leonard. All the way over he's cracking jokes.

"Where's this station at?" he says. "Pittsburgh?" Or: "You gotta be a midget to ride in this Toyota." One line after another.

Finally he wants to know who is the biggest name at the station. At that time it was Martin Agronsky, the political commentator. He had pretty big credentials—NBC, CBS, network correspondent—still does, in fact.

"Oh, yeah," Leonard says. "I remember Martin. He's a good friend of mine. Take me to him."

Now there's one thing about Martin Agronsky off the air. He can be so intense he doesn't seem to see you. He's someone who always seems to be thinking. Not rude or anything, just preoccupied. So Leonard says, "Take me to him." We get off the elevator, go down the hall, and knock on Agronsky's door. He's on the phone. You can hear him talking. He gets up from his desk, opens the door, sees that it's us, and slowly pushes the door closed in our faces. It was funny. He was in a trance. I don't think he knew he was shutting the door.

Well, Leonard couldn't believe it. He was infuriated. Agronsky closed the door in his face.

It is now two minutes till air time and Leonard is going crazy. "Hey, who does Agronsky think he is? I knew him when he was a fly. Who does he think he is? Martin Agronsky, he's nothing, I remember him when he was working at a newsstand in Chicago. Who does he think he is, shutting the door in my face?" He keeps this up all the way down on the elevator, onto the set, and right up to air time. Finally we're on the air.

"Ladies and gentlemen," I say, "we have with us this afternoon one of the greatest comedians of all time, Jack E. Leonard. Jack, how ya' doin'?"

He hardly misses a beat. "Who does Martin Agronsky think he is?" he yells. "I knew him when he was a fly. I knew him when he couldn't bat an eyelash. Martin Agronsky, he's a zero. I know him. What's he doin', shuttin' the door in my face?"

It was amazing. Jack E. Leonard rips Martin Agronsky for fifteen minutes without taking a breath. The viewers must have thought it was a joke. They switch on their sets and—BOOM!—here's Leonard calling Agronsky a fly. All the station officials began coming into the studio. After a while they brought Agronsky down. But it was too late for an apology from Agronsky for shutting the door in Leonard's face. It was 5 p.m. and the show was over.

I don't know why, but boxers often make the best interviews. Maybe it's because they're individuals. No teamwork required. Individuals. One guy like this was Archie Moore, the former light-heavyweight champion. He was terrific. Forty-five years old, gray hair, his belly jiggling over his belt. He was one of the greatest light-heavyweight champions of all time.

The thing that always amazed me was how he could control his weight. To fight as a light-heavyweight, he couldn't come in over 175 pounds. But when he wasn't fighting, you'd see pictures of him and it was obvious he had ballooned to over 200. In the early 1970s, when he was close to 60, he came through Washington. I had him on my show.

"Archie," I said, "what was your secret? How did you always make the 175-pound weight?"

He demonstrated by chewing an imaginary piece of steak. He chewed, and chewed, mouth closed, making a big lump in his cheek.

Every once in a while he'd take an imaginary gulp. ''It's simple, Warner,'' he said. ''I chew my food, steaks, carrots and all. Then I swallow the juices and spit out the food. You lose weight in a hurry if you don't swallow the pulp. The juices are enough to keep you going.''

In December 1958, when he was already 45, Moore had a fight against a guy named Yvon Durelle in Montreal. I watched it on television. We used to have one of those old Zenith sets with the round screen. Durelle knocks old Archie down four times inside the first five rounds—three times in the first round and once in the fifth. Moore can hardly get off his knees. I thought, ''Well, this is going to be it. Archie's going to lose his title.'' You know what happens? Moore comes back and knocks out Durelle in the eleventh round. One of the greatest boxing comebacks I've ever seen in my life. Here's a 45-year-old guy, down four times and on the verge of losing his title, and he comes back and KOs a younger man who is a pretty good fighter.

''I'm going to tell you something funny about that fight,'' Archie says. ''My wife was given a seat right behind Yvon Durelle's corner. That's where they sat her—right in back of Durelle. Now each time after I was knocked down and went to my corner between rounds, I wanted my wife to know I was OK. So I'd give her a little wave as if to say, 'I'm all right, baby.'

''I think this wavin' helped me win the fight. It drove Durelle crazy. He thought I was waving at *him*. The next day after the fight all he wanted to know was, 'How come you were waving at me between rounds? What were you trying to prove?' Man, I wasn't provin' nothin'. I was just wavin' to my baby. Durelle couldn't get over it. I think it did psychological damage to him. During the fight he was sayin', 'Geez, I put this guy down four times, for cryin' out loud, and he's wavin' at me. He must be crazy!' ''

I have a theory about what separates the truly great coach or player from the merely excellent one. Sure, talent counts. So does attitude. But you know what sets Jack Nicklaus, Sandy Koufax, Ted Williams, and guys like that apart from others? They all have incredible concentration and they are perfectionists. A certain number of guys have unbelievable talent. But only a certain number of those are fanatical about detail. Everything must be *just so*. Nothing escapes their attention.

Lombardi was like that. So were two other coaches I've talked to—Don Shula and George Allen. It's not just their minds or their theories that make them great. It's detail.

Let me give you a little story about Shula. The Redskins are playing the Dolphins in an exhibition game, in Tampa, 1969. I'm doing the game for Channel 9 with Ray Scott. The players are going through drills a half-hour before game time, so Ray says let's go down to the field and meet Shula. Ray knew him. ''Coach, I'd like you to meet Warner Wolf, WTOP,'' he says. Now remember, this is only thirty minutes before game time. You'd think Shula had other things to worry about. But before Scott finishes the intro Shula starts staring at my lapel. ''Ladybug,'' he says. He walks right up, grabs the lapel, and flicks the bug off with his thumb and middle finger. It was like, ''Uh, oh, a bug! Better take care of this detail right now.'' Now I don't know, but I'll bet you anything that Don Shula has everything in order. He doesn't keep a messy garage. He's a perfectionist. That's why he's a cut above the others.

It was the same thing with Allen. Once I interviewed him at Redskin Park, a new practice facility he built for the team in the northern Virginia countryside. The carpet man had just been there. Gold wall-to-wall carpet throughout the whole place, just like the team colors. ''You know why I insisted on wall-to-wall?'' he said. ''I had a player in Los Angeles once who tripped on the stairs and tore a ligament because the rugs weren't nailed down. That's the thing with throw rugs. They're not trip-proof.''

The guy thought of everything. I considered him one of the greatest coaches of all time—the best motivator I ever saw. He knew who needed the money to get up and who needed the rah-rah stuff. The old guys worshiped him. He took advantage of every tool at his disposal. Who's a better trader in the NFL than George Allen? Who could get Billy Kilmer for relatively nothing, or Ken Houston, one of the greatest safety men in the history of football? He is not coaching in the NFL and I think football is the poorer for it. He also, however, has a reputation for spending too much of the owners' money.

Toward the end of his career, critics used to make fun of Allen for his psychological ploys. But the guy was brilliant. He was ahead of most coaches. Take the special teams for kickoffs and punts. Until Allen put an emphasis on specialty teams, specialty teams were made up of guys who were demoted, or rookies. Allen's special teams had a special captain and a special purpose. He made those guys feel important to the point where they won ball games.

"Hey, coach, who are you going to introduce this week, offense or defense?"

"Neither. We're going to introduce Rusty Tillman and the special teams."

Fantastic!

Then there was one of the greatest emotional coups I've seen in sports. The Redskins are playing the Cowboys in the National Football Conference championship game, New Year's Eve, 1972. National television, 4 o'clock. The winner goes to the Super Bowl to play undefeated Miami, who beat Pittsburgh earlier that day. The game is being played in Washington, but Dallas is the favorite because everybody knows the Cowboys win the big ones.

I'm sitting in the upper deck. The Cowboys take the field about five minutes to four, so the game can start on time for television. Slowly it dawns on the crowd that there are no Redskins. The tension starts building. It's like "C'mon, c'mon, where are they? Let's see 'em!" And finally, at approximately ten minutes after four, "Yahhhhhhhh! There they are!" It was unbelievable. Allen had held the Redskins in the locker room. By the time the Redskins took the field, the anticipation was so high people were ready to keel over. The fans knew what was happening, which made it even better. When the Redskins came out, it was like a tidal wave being unleashed on the Cowboys. You could see them shrink. The fans knew what they were expected to do. Allen wanted them to make the Redskins feel invincible—and they did!

Although they trailed only 10–3 at halftime, the Cowboys were never really in the game. Total wipeout, 26–3. I can't remember a crucial game such as this before or since in which the Cowboys were so completely outplayed and outcoached. The defense killed Roger Staubach. Absolutely mauled him. Billy Kilmer threw two touchdowns to Charley Taylor and Curt Knight kicked four field goals. From the moment the Redskins took the field there was never any doubt who was going to win. And the guy who gave the Redskins a psychological advantage was Allen. Ironically, ten years later, same field, same NFC championship, the Skins beat the Cowboys again, 31–17.

I will say this: Allen was a master—of media as well as his players. Win or lose, he would always be there on Monday morning. He would not duck the press. But he might dodge your questions. He was like a politician this way. You'd try to pin him down and forget it, he'd change the subject without batting an eyelash. He'd try to make you believe he was answering the question you asked. But what he really was doing was answering the question *he* wanted to hear.

Early in the 1972 Super Bowl season, Kilmer started a game against the Patriots and played fairly well. But toward the end the Patriots took the lead, 24–23. Kilmer went cold. He was 0 for 8 down the stretch, although in all fairness to Kilmer, two passes were dropped, including one for a touchdown. The obvious question was, why didn't Allen yank Kilmer and put in Sonny Jurgensen? I didn't want to make Kilmer look bad and I wasn't out to get Allen, so I put it diplomatically.

"Coach," I said, "how come you didn't bring in Sonny as they do in baseball when the starting pitcher runs out of steam?" Allen loved baseball terminology, so I threw in some stuff about bull pens and relievers being ready. I figured he'd start talking.

No way. He knew it was a no-win question. There was a Billy-versus-Sonny rivalry at the time. Most of the fans were for Sonny, and Allen didn't want to intensify it.

"You know, Warner," he said, "football is not like baseball. We don't have relief pitchers in football."

"I know you don't call 'em that, coach, but isn't that what they really are?'' Allen insisted you could not compare a relief pitcher with a substitute Q.B.

Another time the Redskins and the Eagles started throwing punches at each other. ''Coach,'' I said, ''what about these fights? Whaddya think of 'em?''

''Look,'' he said, ''that shows these guys are aggressive. It's all right with me. In Los Angeles, I used to suggest that guys maybe do get in a couple fights, just to show they're not lazy and sitting back and taking the paycheck.''

I went with it. Top of the show. I showed the tape of Allen saying that sometimes fighting is all right. The next time I see Allen he comes up to me with a sheepish look, like the kid who just came back from the principal's office. ''Geez, Warner, you got me in trouble by playing that piece we did. The league called me up. They frown on that kind of stuff, you know.'' He wouldn't say, but I think they gave him a fine.

I could never understand the knock on Allen. People said, ''Sure, he wins, but he's traded away all our draft choices.'' To me, that complaint made no sense. It's like somebody saying, ''Yeah, he's made a lot of money now, but how is he going to make it in the future?'' Come on, the man won. He was in the playoffs five out of seven years in Washington. He was in the Super Bowl. And yet people were knocking him for the future, which no one can predict. To me, it was a narrow-minded attitude. Come on! The guy's taking you to the Super Bowl and you're worried about what's going to happen in five years?

In November 1972 I was playing touch football with some friends at Churchill High School in Potomac, Maryland. I'm running the ball and—BOOM!—I feel like somebody has kicked me in the back of my heel. I turn around and there's nobody there. Then I look at my foot, which is just dangling there. I had snapped my Achilles tendon, just like Jurgensen had done two weeks before in Yankee Stadium. The great part about it is that I'm in Suburban Hospital a few days later when I get this telegram. ''Dear Warner,'' it says, ''because of your Achilles tendon injury I have no recourse except to put you on the injured reserve list. Your friend, George Allen.''

Those Channel 9 years were great. After WTOP lost the Redskin exhibition games, every team I touched turned into garbage. It was amazing. I think I must hold the record for most consecutive losses by an announcer. The final year of the Senators, they lost almost every road game we did. I had done Maryland football in 1967 and they were 0–9. In 1974–75 I was the first color announcer for the Washington Capitals. We did something like twenty-five road games and they went 0–25. They were the worst hockey team in history, winning only 8 out of 80 games all year.

One story I'm not proud of took place in Boston in 1974. I was doing a Celtics-Bullets game from the Boston Garden—same booth I had been in eight years earlier for the Celtics-Lakers seventh game on radio. The Bullets had moved from Baltimore to Washington the year before, so the telecast was being sent back to both cities. I'm up there in the booth with Chuck Taylor, my announcing partner, and my wife, Sue, who's standing off camera with the producer.

Now there's one thing you must understand about the Boston Garden. You're high up. Third balcony. During the halftime, there's no time for the players to come to the booth for interviews. You have to do down to the floor yourself and corral them. This particular night, Chuck says he's going to try to get Mike Riordan of the Bullets. Failing Riordan he'd try for Elvin Hayes. Toward the end of the half he waves so long and starts down.

The Garden is an old place with lots of back staircases. It must have taken Chuck longer than he thought. By the time he gets halfway down, the half ends. Intermission. Everybody pours into the aisles and goes up and down the staircases for hot dogs. By the time Taylor gets to the floor, Riordan and Hayes are long gone. So the producer throws the show back to me for the halftime. "Fill! Fill!" he yells in my ear.

Ordinarily, there would have been no problem. I would have gone over the stats and then talked about Washington sports. But this game was also going back to Baltimore. People in Baltimore didn't care about Washington sports. So after I did the stats and told the cameraman to shoot the Celtic championship flags hanging from the roof of the Garden, I had nothing left. Ten minutes to go, zero material, and they're still yelling "Fill!"

Now here's where I went wrong. I was desperate, and it just so happened my wife is sitting next to me in the booth.

"Folks, this is my wife, Sue," I said.

It was unfair. She's waving me off. No way she wants to be on camera.

"C'mon, c'mon!" I say.

"Warner," she says, "I'm going to kill you."

But I had no choice.

"How do you like Boston?" I asked her.

"Very nice. Very nice."

"Pretty good game, huh?"

"Yes it is. Very exciting."

"You have a nice time up here today seeing Boston?"

It went on like this for what seemed like an eternity. *Boo* on me! I was asking the worst questions of all time. She'd try to respond, but there was nothing to respond to. She was mortified. I was dying. It was terrible judgment on my part.

At last, with two minutes to go before the second half starts, Chuck Taylor runs down Mike Riordan of the Bullets, who are coming back on the court. "Well, hon," I say, "I see Chuck finally has his guest. Let's go down to the floor and talk with Mike Riordan." *Whew!* Was I ever glad that was over! Terrible! Worst ten minutes I ever spent on camera. And it was all my fault. I remember at the end of that year a columnist in the *Washington Post* wrote a piece about New Year's resolutions. There it was, right at the top: "Warner Wolf promises never to interview his wife again on television."

I had another bad experience that year, but at least this was funnier.

April 1974. I'm doing the color on the new Washington Capitals hockey games. They're playing the Red Wings in Detroit on a Wednesday night. I fly out of Washington that afternoon and it's sunny and 50° in Washington. I've got a leisure suit on. Open shirt, the whole works. You'd think it was Florida. I arrive in Detroit and I can tell it's colder, maybe 35°.

"All right," I think, "so what, I'm going to ride to the arena in a rental car. I'll be inside, so it won't matter."

I get off the plane, rent a car, start driving to Olympia Stadium, and turn on the radio.

"Snow warning!" the guy says.

I actually start talking back to the guy. "Snow? Come on, man, this is April! Thirty-five degrees. How can there be snow?"

I get to the Detroit Olympia at 6 o'clock and go inside. Game's over at 11 o'clock. I come outside and it's just like the guy said. Gigantic snowstorm in Detroit. The temperature has gone down to 25°. It must have snowed five inches in five hours.

I'm standing there at the exit gate ready to go into the parking lot to get my car, with all the other people, when I realize every car in the lot is covered with snow. They all look the same. When you rent a car, who remembers to look at the color or the make? And even if I could remember, all the cars were covered with snow.

First I go into the lot, wiping the snow off license plates, trying to match the license plates with the number on my keys. No good. Plus I'm freezing with my leisure suit on.

You know what I had to do? I had to wait from 11 p.m. to 12:30 in the morning for every other car to leave the lot, so that the remaining car would be my car. Horrible. I watch every player leave. Popcorn vendors, the guy who drives the Zamboni machine, writers, refs, security men. I watch every one of them go.

Finally, it got down to about eight cars and I was the only guy left. I guess some people figured it wasn't worth it and took the bus home. Now remember, this is April. Leisure suit. I take my key out and start wading through the snow, sticking the key in every door. Bad, man. It's up to my knees. No boots. The snow is caked all over my pants.

After about fifteen minutes the key works in one of the car doors. It's my car! I had to brush the snow off the windshield with my sleeve. What a night! It just so happened, it was the last hockey game I ever did.

7

Questions from the Fans

When I was 7 years old, my father began buying me *Ring* magazine . . . boxing, my first love.

Well, over the years a lot of people have asked me how I would rank the all-time heavyweight fighters. "Where do you put Ali?" they say. A lot of younger people have seen Ali, but they didn't see the other guys. Personally, among the fighters I have seen, I have to go with Joe Louis first, Ali second, and Marciano third. Except for films, I never saw Jack Johnson, who won the title in 1908. However, from what I've read and from the films that I've watched, Johnson was the first real defensive heavyweight champion we had and a great counter-puncher.

But there's no getting around Louis. Not only was he a great boxer, but he could also knock you out with either hand. Now I'm not putting down Ali, but most of his wins were *technical* knockouts, not pure knockouts. In other words, the referee often stopped Ali's fights because his opponent was taking too much punishment. With Louis, they were clear knockouts. He hit you, the referee counted ten, and the fight was over. Louis would stalk his opponent and then BOOM! one punch, either hand, and it's all over. He could knock you out with a left or a right. With Ali, when he did knock out his opponents, it usually took a series of punches to do it.

Unlike a lot of fighters, Louis also knew how to finish you off. If he caught you and you were in trouble, you might as well say good night. The fight would be over. You would not escape. Once he measured you, that fight was going to be over in the next thirty seconds. Today, too many fighters will stagger a guy and let the guy get away. They don't know the art of finishing off their opponents.

Louis also could take a punch. In eighteen years of fighting, from 1934 to 1951, he was knocked out only twice—by Max Schmeling in 1936 and Rocky Marciano in 1951. Plus Louis held the title longer than any other heavyweight champion. Eleven years, eight months, and one week. And during those years he was not an idle champion. He defended his title a record twenty-five times.

Ali vs. Marciano. First I think of the terrible number of punches Ali would have landed! I'm inclined to think Marciano couldn't have endured that kind of punishment. But then I remember how he beat Ezzard Charles after taking all those punches. You've also got to add in the fact that Ali was really a TKO puncher and might not have been able to take Marciano out.

It seems to me they would have split the first two fights and Ali would have won a third fight because of his speed. Overall, speed would have counted for more in the scoring than Marciano's endurance.

My reasoning is there's a parallel between Marciano and Joe Frazier, who beat Ali once and lost to him twice. Marciano and Frazier both were body punchers. They kept boring in. They paid a price for every punch they landed. But they made you pay, too, because they were devastating punchers. So I think Marciano could have beaten Ali at least one time.

Rating the quarterbacks is easier. People say, who's the greatest you ever saw? I saw Sammy Baugh at the end of his career in Washington. I saw Y. A. Tittle with the '49ers and the Giants. I saw Otto Graham play ten years for the Browns and win ten NFL or All-America Football Conference division titles or championship games—ten for ten. I saw Fran Tarkenton and Sonny Jurgensen, Bart Starr and Joe Namath. I've seen Terry Bradshaw and Roger Staubach. But if I had to pick one guy to win one game, it would be Johnny Unitas. I can remember too many times, week after week over a twelve-year period, when the Colts would be behind in the fourth quarter and Unitas always seemed to bring 'em back. Sure, he had good material. But he was the guy who threw the passes. One of his strong points: He would hold the ball until the last possible second before releasing it, and then get clobbered still completing the pass. I remember the Colt-Packer game in Baltimore in 1965. Packers lead 10–0, two minutes to go, Unitas takes 'em downfield twice, hits Willie Richardson, and the Colts win 13–10.

Jurgensen rates high because of what he did with no running game and no defense. He'd keep the Redskins in games they had no business being in. Typical Redskin game, Redskins–Browns, 1967, in Cleveland, Jergy helps the Skins put 37 points on the board, but the Skins lose 42–37. Namath? One of the best arms in football. But keep in mind that when he first started, he played in the American Football League, and they didn't play great defense. Plus Namath got maximum mileage out of that one Super Bowl game against the Colts in 1969. Bradshaw and Stauback? Certainly two of the greatest money players of all time. *Winners*.

Another question I still hear in Washington and New York is: Where do you draw the line on teams moving to other cities? New York lost the Brooklyn Dodgers and the New York Giants more than twenty-five years ago, but it still bothers people. Washington lost the Senators twice, in 1961 and 1972. Boston and Milwaukee lost the Braves. St. Louis lost the Browns. Philadelphia lost the A's and Seattle lost the Pilots.

In any other business, if a guy wants to move to another corner because he's not making it, that's it. It doesn't matter if he has a vegetable stand or a steel company. He moves. That's the freedom of this country. But on the other hand—here's where I draw the line—there's a social responsibility in owning a team. If the city supports the product in proportion to its value, then moving is wrong. To me, if you're winning and nobody's coming out, then go ahead, pack up and hit the road. But if you're not putting a good product on the field, you can't complain about attendance. You have no right to move if your product is rotten and fails to draw what you think it should.

Bob Short's last year in Washington was 1971. He drew 655,000 people. But he had a terrible team. Look at the record. The Senators were 63–96, 38½ games out of first. What did he expect to draw with a club like that? No way he had a right to move.

It was the same thing in 1960, Calvin Griffith's final year. He drew 743,000 fans in a stadium that seated 29,000. He should cry about that? Come on, that was all that he deserved to draw. The Senators were a bad team, 73–81, 24 games behind the Yankees. The annoying part was, you could see the Senators were improving. The fans had supported them when they were bad and now they were about to blossom. So what did Griffith do? He moved them to Minnesota to reap the harvest. The guy wanted to make a killing. Same thing with Walter O'Malley and the Dodgers. The fans had supported the Dodgers in Brooklyn. It's just that O'Malley wanted to make more.

Now the hard part is that it cuts both ways. If the team is winning and you don't draw, then fans can't complain if you move. The Pirates are a case in point. I'm not wishing this on Pittsburgh, but it seems to me the Galbreath family has every right to move. The Pirates are always competitive but they don't draw beans. Neither do the Baltimore Orioles. They've been the winningest team in the American League over the past eleven years in total games. They should draw 2 million year after year, but they don't.

Another question people ask: Don't you agree these ball players are getting paid too much? My answer is, be fair. They are performers. If people are willing to pay X number of dollars to see them, then they should make X number of dollars in return. People spend lots of money at the movie theater, but who complains when Robert Redford makes a million? Why should they complain when Dave Winfield makes a million? The traditional view is that players should be treated one way and movie stars another. Come on, that's not right. Both are performers in the entertainment business. The owners will charge what people will pay. Why should the owners be the only ones who profit?

How about the 1982 NFL strike? I couldn't believe the players were asking for a percentage of the business. That would be like me asking CBS for a percentage of their profit. No way. The owners are the employers and the players are the employees.

However, since pro football is the number one team spectator sport in the United States, I feel the players should be paid accordingly. Instead, the average salary of basketball, baseball, and hockey players is higher than football players. That's not right. It's true that NFL players play only sixteen regular season games, much less than the other three sports. However, unlike baseball, basketball, and hockey, a football player risks permanent injury on every play and his average life span in the NFL is only $4^1/_2$ years.

The trouble with baseball is that it's traditional where it should be in favor of change, and it changes where it should be traditional. Uniforms, for example. When I grew up, the home team wore white, the road team wore gray. That was it. Every team's home uniform was the same, except for the insignia and except for the Yankees, who had pinstripes. You could always count on what the uniforms looked like. Washington had a big "W" on the left side of the chest. Chicago had the letters "SOX" overlapping down the front. It was a stable world. Now you never know which uniform they're going to wear. Red shirts at night, orange shirts in the afternoon. Blue pants, pullovers. Take a look at the Pirates' uniforms. They look like softball uniforms. And the Astros' uniforms—bad news, man.

Another point where baseball's logic is backwards is the foul pole. Why do they call it the foul pole and the foul line when it should be the fair pole and the fair line? If a ball hits the foul pole or the foul line, it's a fair ball, not a foul ball. So obviously, it should be called the fair pole or the fair line. If you want to call it the foul pole, make it a foul ball when the ball hits it. Try to explain to someone just learning the game that when a ball hits the foul line, it's fair. Come on, give us a break!

Then there are the parks. Baseball is tearing down the old parks, the ones where you were closest to the players. If you want to tear down parks, go after the big stadiums that all look alike. When I was in Fenway Park in Boston or Tiger Stadium in Detroit, it was never boring. But it was a different story in places like Cincinnati,

Pittsburgh, St. Louis, and Philadelphia. If somebody woke you up in the middle of one of those four stadiums and asked you where you were, you wouldn't know. They all look the same.

I'll tell you a story about being close to the field. Everybody remembers the Yankees' famous brawl at the Copacabana nightclub in 1957, involving Billy Martin, Mickey Mantle, and Hank Bauer. It resulted in Martin being traded to Kansas City. A few weeks later, Mantle and the Yankees came to Griffith Stadium. We're in the bleachers, right in back of Mantle in center field. He had to feel bad about Martin, his pal, getting traded. So we rubbed it in. "C'mon, Mickey, let's go, big party tonight at the Hayloft [which at the time was a local rock 'n roll bar in Washington]! Come on, you, Martin, and us! After the game, we'll buy the first round!"

He acted like he didn't hear us, but he had to, he was only 100 feet away. Finally we say, "C'mon, Mickey, how about a picture?" We put our cameras up, ready for the shot. You know what he does? He bends over and shakes his backside at us. We all gave Mantle a hand. What a great sport!

The point is that he was close enough to shut *us* up. At Griffith Stadium the players and the fans could talk to each other. That's why Fenway is so great. Wow, what a quaint little place! The streets are nice around it, right downtown, plenty of transportation. The key is that you can reach out and touch the players. The short left field wall with the screen on top of it seems like it's just in back of third base. And still they have a guy who puts up the numbers in the scoreboard by hand. Sometimes you can see a hand with a one or two and up goes the score.

Another thing is that the outfield distances of Fenway are not uniform. You never get bored announcing there because somebody can always score. There's a constant sense of anticipation. Also, you learn something new about Fenway every time. I remember the night I found out about the hot dogs sold by the vendor at the hot dog stand on the left field roof. Even though newspaper, TV, and radio men and women can eat free in the press room, after I found out about the hot dogs on the roof, I never ate in the press room again; I went straight for the hot dogs on the left field roof. Great rolls, tasty mustard, and *hot* hot dogs. You can't beat a good hot dog at the ball park.

Detroit is another great place to do a game. A double-decked stadium with center field bleachers. Everything's deep green. The players are so close you can hear them chatter. They still have the small auxiliary scoreboard out in left field at ground level. Plus the broadcast booth actually hangs over the field. You could look right down on the third base coach's cap. If he took it off, you could tell whether or not he had a bald spot.

One of the great things about Baltimore is the press room. The only city in both leagues to have crab cakes. Man are they great! Bloomington, Minnesota, the old home of the Twins, used to be nice because you could see a silo over left field and farm lands beyond that. It was clean. A great breath of open-air scenery. But now they've moved to a big dome the Twins share with the Vikings. Until the mid-1960s Shibe Park in Philadelphia, later named Connie Mack Stadium, was a great park. The bull pen in right field had to be some kind of a joke. The pitchers warmed up in this little wedge of a space between the foul line and the right field stands. When left-handers got up to throw a curve, they were so close to the wall, they used to say they scraped their knuckles on the wall while warming up. Philadelphia ripped the place down and now, of course, play in Veterans' Stadium. They do have some picnic tables and potted plants down the foul lines there, but as I say, it's more or less like Pittsburgh, St. Louis, or Cincinnati.

A strange feeling is the Astrodome in Houston. I never got used to it. One of the weirdest feelings I ever had. You know you are inside the dome, so there is no way you have that stretch-out-and-breathe feeling. No open air. It is like "Gimme some room! What is this, the Twilight Zone?" The sounds were even different. I guess if you were there every game for a whole year, maybe you'd get used to it. But the noises aren't right. You know the sound of a bat hitting a ball in the open air? In the Astrodome, it is a dull, hollow sound.

Bad as they are, Cincinnati and Houston have nothing on Cleveland Municipal Stadium. In my opinion it's the worst ball park in the league for baseball. You can have 18,000 people there and it looks like there are 1,800. It's so mammoth, it's ridiculous. It's supposed to hold 76,000 but the Indians average about 10,000. So the players are usually playing before 66,000 empty seats. Think how this feels. If 10,000 are there, almost seven-eighths of the place is empty. Plus the stands and the announcing booth are miles away from the field. Ted Williams used to say that it's a heck of a lot easier to play before 50,000 fans than before 5,000 fans. Maybe that's one reason the Indians keep losing year after year.

Comiskey Park, Chicago, is a great place. Big square park and you're still close to the players. The pitchers warm up in front of the box seats. You get an open feeling because the park has archways behind the left and right field stands. You can see the trees through the left field arches, and the sun comes through late in the day. The big attraction when I went there, though, was Bill Veeck. He is one of the greatest owners who ever lived. For one thing, he's the only man I know whose office had no walls and no doors. You walked in, there he was, right out in the front room. "I don't believe in doors," he said. "I've got nothing to hide. If the people want to come and see me, let 'em come and see me. It's good for employees, too. I want them to feel they can walk in here any time."

Veeck was show business. That's what put him ahead of everybody else. He knew baseball was show business before these other guys did, and he would admit it. What an imagination he had. Over the years, he would let all the barbers in for free one night and all the taxi drivers in the next. He had dairy night. *Milk the cow in the fastest time and win a trip to Puerto Rico*. Exploding scoreboard. Sirens when you hit a homer. *Ten-thousandth fan in gate wins Cadillac*. He knew he had to give the fans something, not the other way around. If they had a good time, they would come back. In 1951, when he owned the Browns in St. Louis, he put Eddie Gaedel, the midget, up to bat. Bob Cain walked him on four pitches. Baseball management thought that was terrible. I thought it was great. I respect Bill Veeck.

When I was calling a Senators game from Chicago, I went to see Veeck for my television show. He's always good for an anecdote. "Warner," he said, "let me show you how backward some of my fellow owners are." He took out some papers that were signed by his father, Bill Veeck, Sr., when he owned the Chicago Cubs in 1922. The papers were a well-reasoned argument for inter-league play with the American League.

"See this?" Veeck said. "My colleagues try to tell you that inter-league play is some crazy new idea. My father was promoting it in the National League half a century ago. That's how long baseball has resisted."

Veeck was the American League's strongest supporter of inter-league play. He had some backing within the AL. It's too bad the National League slammed the door in his face. The NL felt it had a superior product and didn't need the AL. Baseball is the poorer now that Veeck has retired and is no longer pushing this issue.

With Hall of Fame center fielder Joe DiMaggio, "a class guy" (June 1980)

With three of New York's greatest Center Fielders of the 1950s: Mickey Mantle, Yankees (left), Duke Snider (center), and Willie Mays, Giants (right). October 1981, "The Warner Wolf Show" WCBS-TV

With 1979 World Series Most Valuable Player, Willie Stargell of the championship team, the Pittsburgh Pirates.

With Paul Newman, who takes his race car driving seriously. April 1982. (*Associated Press photo by Dave Pickoff*)

With two of the greatest fighters, Gene Tunney and Jack Dempsey, at the National Press Club in 1965.

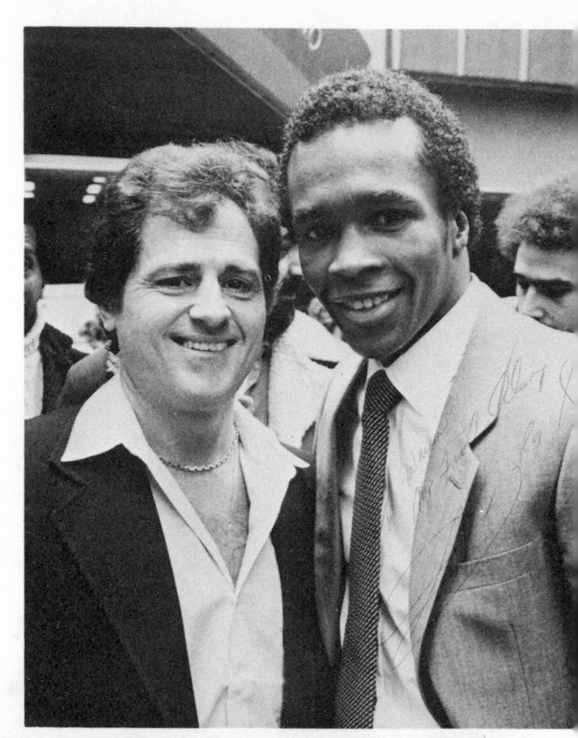

The duel of the crutches with Hall of Fame quarterback Sonny Jurgensen of the Redskins. In October 1979, Jurgensen had broken his Achilles tendon in a game against the Giants; two weeks later in a touch football game, Warner had broken his. (*Nate Fine*)

(*Top, Facing Page*) With former Welterweight champion Sugar Ray Leonard. Sugar Ray grew up in the Washington, D.C. area and as a youngster used to listen to Warner on the radio. (*UPI photo*)

(*Bottom, Facing Page*) At surprise birthday party for Muhammad Ali in New York City, January 1979. Ali was 37.

With Redskin coach, George Allen, in April 1971, his first year in Washington. The next season he took the Skins to the Superbowl. (*Nate Fine*)

As M.C. at halftime of Redskin game on Bobby Mitchell Day, 1969, just after Mitchell, a Hall of Famer, retired. Ethel Kennedy (left), Mitchell, his wife Gwynn and their two children. (*Nate Fine*)

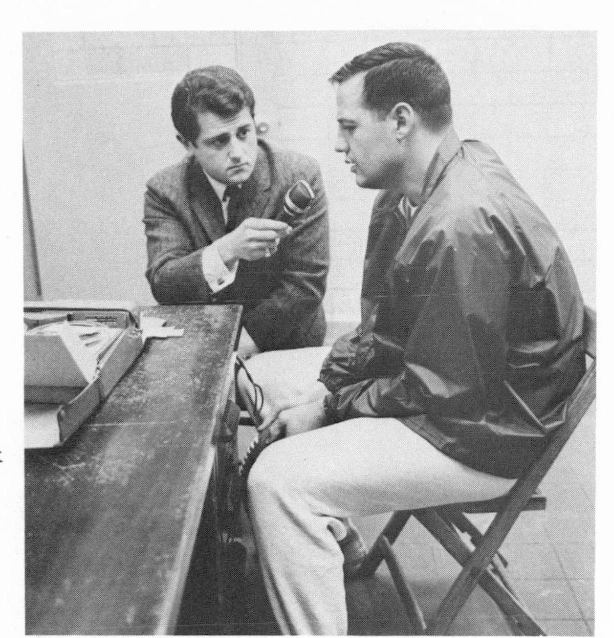

With Hall-of-Fame linebacker, Sam Huff. Huff retired from the Redskins in 1967, but came back in 1969 to play one year under Vince Lombardi.

With Hall-of-Famer Al Kaline (left) and the late Jesse Owens (right) at WTOP Radio Station in Washington, D.C., 1968. (*Courtesy WTOP*)

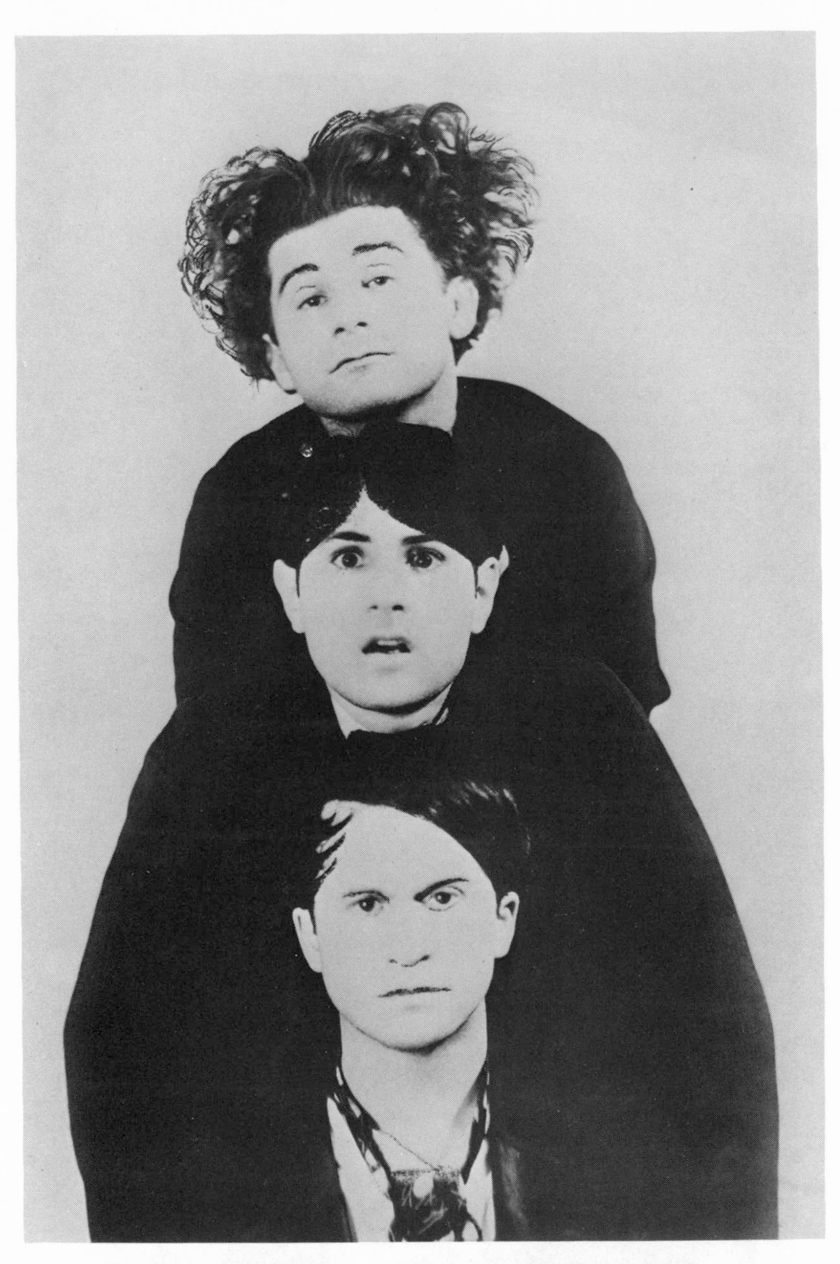

Ted Healy's STOOGES in a 1933 vaudeville act at the Palladium in London.

Mousie Garner (top), Jack Wolf (middle), Warner's father, and Dick Hakins

8

The Boos of the Week

I've come up with a few "Boos of the Week," some of which I've delivered on television and some of which I haven't. To me, the lack of inter-league play has got to be at the top of the list.

Boo on the owners!

Inter-league play is a must. In every other sport, everybody plays everybody. NFL, NBA, NHL. Get rid of this National League East, American League West nonsense. Realign the leagues in the interest of rivalries. There's no more National and American. That's gone. It's East Division, West Division, Southwest, Midwest. That's it. Total realignment. If you want to give the divisions titles, go ahead, I don't care. The names don't matter. All the fans are interested in are the rivalries.

The Yankees would play the Mets, the White Sox would play the Cubs, the Dodgers would play the Angels: Astros–Rangers, Giants–A's. Are you kidding? This would be tremendous. It's a natural. Plus it would save the owners travel expenses. I can't believe the owners don't go for it.

Just break the league up into four divisions, two divisions of six and two divisions of seven. The four winners play and that's it. Division I plays Division II, Division III plays Division IV, the two survivors go to the World Series. Nothing complex about it.

♦ ♦ ♦

Boo on old-fashioned baseball rules!

I've got two thoughts here. First, let's say the visiting team trails, 2–1, top of the ninth inning. First batter gets on. Does the team bunt and move the runner down to second? No, they hit away! All because there's an old baseball axiom that says you must play to win on the road and play to tie at home. That's baloney! What's wrong with trying to tie the game on the road? You have to tie the game before you can win it. Tie the game in the top of the ninth, and hope you hold 'em and win it in extra innings.

You follow that? It's so archaic, it's ridiculous!

The second thing is postponing an incomplete game and starting from scratch. For example, let's say the Mets lead the Padres 3–1. Dave Kingman has hit two home runs for the Mets. The Padres are up with two outs in the top of the fifth and the rains come down. Two hours later, the game is called: "Postponed—rain." None of the records count. They start from scratch because the game didn't go at least 4½ innings.

That's a bad rule. Why should Kingman be penalized and cheated out of his two home runs just because it rained? He hit 'em, and they should count. Pick up the game where you left off. In golf, if everybody else is finished but five guys are still on the course when it rains, everybody elses's rounds count and those other five guys complete their rounds the next day. They don't start from scratch. Same thing with tennis. If half the guys finish and it rains, the guys who didn't finish complete their matches the next day, they don't start from scratch. Baseball should do the same thing.

Boo on Bowie!

Another *boo* goes to baseball commissioner Bowie Kuhn, who over the last three years has banned both Mickey Mantle and Willie Mays from being employed by baseball, after both Mantle and Mays were hired by Atlantic City hotel casinos. What a double standard! It's OK for baseball owners to own racehorses but not OK for Mantle and Mays to work for hotel casinos. Gambling is gambling. What's the difference if it's at the race track or at the casino?

Mr. Kuhn's rationale is that some of the owners and players already owned the racehorses before he came into office. Weak argument. It seems to me it's either OK for both the owners and Mantle and Mays, or it's wrong for both the owners and Mantle and Mays. But it can't be right for one and wrong for the other. *Boo* on Bowie.

Boo on artificial turf!

Man, is this stuff bad. The ultimate phoniness. One of the greatest things you could do was go to a night game and see the green grass. It was honest green. You could see the dew on it. Now it's got seams and zippers, and they use a Zamboni machine to clear the water off it. Come on, get rid of all this fakery. Give me real grass. Bring back the dirt base paths instead of having these sliding patches.

An even better reason for getting rid of artificial turf is the injuries. No one can tell me it doesn't cut down on players' careers. I've seen what it does. These athletes take an unbelievable amount of punishment. I remember once I was interviewing Mike Bass, a cornerback for the Redskins. I noticed he had open sores on his arms. Nasty looking things, big welts with no skin on them. The guy looked like he should be in a hospital covered with salve.

"Mike," I said, "what are these things?"

"Rug burns. You get 'em from sliding on the carpet. Burns the skin right off. They only heal in the off-season."

The other thing about artificial turf is the hardness of the rug. Larry Brown of the Redskins, who won the NFL rushing title in 1970, once told me that being tackled on the rug was like being tackled on Fifth Avenue. You only have so many falls on the side-walk until you wind up being a cripple. I think it was a blessing for Brown that he played as many games as he did in RFK Stadium, which had real grass. Otherwise his career would have ended even sooner. Whenever Brown played on natural grass, he was as happy as a little kid. In the final game of the year in 1975, the Redskins played the Eagles in the snow at RFK. Brown said it reminded him of being a youngster in Pittsburgh. You could fall on the ground in the snow and not get hurt. Mother Earth. But on artificial turf, there's always pain.

Boo on hockey fights!

There's so much hypocrisy in hockey it's a joke. The owners keep saying they want a clean sport. Baloney! If the owners wanted to stop hockey fights all they would have to do is adopt a very simple rule. Every hockey fight begins the same way. The first thing the players do is throw down their gloves on the ice so they can grab and fight. My rule is easy: *He who throws down his gloves is automatically ejected from the game.*

If you think you can fight with those gloves on, you're not being realistic. You can *try* to fight. You can slap. But fight? No way! First of all, they're too cumbersome to hit anybody with. And second, you can't grab your opponent with one hand and hit him with the other if you have your gloves on. At best, if players kept their gloves on, they would wrestle each other to the ice and there would be no fights.

The beautiful thing is it's a blanket rule: *Take gloves off, out of the game.* Plus you can make the penalty more severe if you wish. Say the guy throws his gloves down and starts fighting with only two minutes to go in the game. "Big deal," he says. "I'm out of the game. So what? There's only two minutes left." Well, you say he's out of this game *and* the next game too for fighting.

That's a pretty simple rule if they really wanted to ban fighting. But the problem is, some of the owners are afraid people will stop coming to the games if there are no fights. This may be true, but for every person who will stop coming to a game because there are no more fights, I believe there are two people who will start showing up.

Boo on the National Hockey League playoffs!

Sixteen out of twenty-one teams are in the National Hockey League playoffs. Come on, give us a break! You play eighty regular-season games to eliminate only five teams? Put a premium on making the playoffs and just take the first eight teams—not sixteen. It makes a complete joke of the regular season. It's like the regular season is nothing more than an eighty-game exhibition season, with the real season being the playoffs.

Boo on boxing titles!

Get rid of this WBA (World Boxing Association) and WBC (World Boxing Council). Down the drain with both of them. Get rid of all these junior, super, and cruiserweight titles. Baloney! All they are are championships to make more money for the WBA, WBC, and TV. The more championships, the more payoffs from television. It's as simple as that. This super/junior/cruiserweight stuff is bad for the fans. It was great in the old days. In the 1940s and 1950s you had eight champions in eight weight divisions. Flyweight, bantomweight, featherweight, lightweight, welterweight, middleweight, light-heavyweight, and heavyweight. Everyone knew who the eight champions were. Now you have over twenty champions. It's watered down. Have the WBA champions fight the WBC champions in each division, and the winner declared world champion. Eight divisions, one champion.

Boo on horse racing for calling itself the number one spectator sport!

Each year the *Daily Racing Form* comes out and tells us that racing attracts more fans than any other sport in the United States. But there's a difference between fans and bettors. What the racing people never tell you is that if there were no betting, it wouldn't even come close to being number one.

I made this point on the air in 1977 when the tellers went on strike at Belmont. The horses still ran, but there was no wagering. I said, "Yesterday, a perfect summer day at Belmont, two thousand people showed up instead of twenty thousand. You're telling me that racing is number one?" Hey, to compare it to other sports, you've got to take away the betting. Or, figure what football, baseball, and basketball would be like if there were legalized betting at the games.

Now there was a guy from Belmont who would call me each

day and give me the results, which I would put on the air. He calls up, and before he tells me the winners he says, "What did you say on the air last night? The New York Racing Association is really upset with you."

I can't believe some people. They don't want to hear the truth. I say that's too bad, as long as I'm fair. They sometimes try to intimidate you when you're on TV, and you can't let 'em.

Boo on the coaches' gag rule!

Every year in the NFL you hear of coaches being fined for criticizing an official's call. George Allen used to draw fines all the time. Don Shula gets them. So did Dick Vermeil and half a dozen other guys. There's something wrong here. Any citizen in the United States can publicly criticize the president of the United States. But an NFL official cannot be criticized. The league thinks criticism will undermine the fans' opinion of the referees. Come on, let the coaches say what they want. We either have freedom of speech in this country or we don't.

Boo on the NFL rules!

Use the two-point conversion in the NFL as it's used in the USFL. Come on, run it in. Pass it in. Two points, it's terrific. What, are you kidding? When the American Football League had it, this was the greatest thing going. It added excitement and suspense. It helps eliminate your overtimes. You wouldn't have as many tie games after the fourth quarter. Think of it: Fourth quarter, one minute left, you trail, 21–14. You score and it's 21–20. Do you go for two points or one? You go for the win and take a chance on losing, or do you go for the tie and overtime?

The only reason I can think why they don't use the two-pointer is the coaches. I once asked Lombardi why the NFL didn't have it while the AFL did. "If I were to answer that honestly," he said, "I'd have to tell you it's because the coaches are opposed. It would put even more pressure on them. They'd have to make more decisions and it would open them up to the second guess."

Another rule they ought to put in is running the ball out of the end zone on kickoffs. Make it mandatory, just like in Canada. No more of these 6-foot-2, 220-pound guys catching the ball in the end zone and then kneeling down. My grandmother could do that. If the guy chooses to down the ball in the end zone instead of running it out, it's a point against his team. In Canada it's called a *rouge* or a single. It's a great rule because it eliminates the single most boring aspect of professional football. Who needs this kneel-down-in-the-end-zone stuff? Don't give the guy an out. Make him run with it—unless, of course, the kickoff goes out of the end zone.

Boo on not using the replay in football.

When you can, use the TV replay to help the officials. Come on, the replay is there. It's not going to go away. You can't ignore it. If the replay shows that the ref is obviously wrong and the replay is not used, it's unfair. It's simple. All you do is give each coach two TV replay time-outs per game. It's up to him when he wants to use them. To keep coaches from using them frivolously, you include a penalty rule. If the coach's viewpoint is proven correct by the replay, fine, the original referee's decision is reversed. But if the coach is proven wrong, he gets hit with a 15-yard penalty. If there is not a clear angle on the TV replay, the play stands as is and there's no penalty.

People say, who will be the judge? Simple. You put an appeals ref up in the booth looking at a monitor. All he would do is rule on challenges. If the cameras showed it, he'd say, "Coach Landry was right, Wilbert Montgomery definitely stepped out of bounds." If the ref checked the replay and Montgomery was not out of bounds, he'd say, "Play stands, Cowboys penalized fifteen yards." The maximum the replay time-outs would hold up the game would be four minutes—one minute for each appeal if both coaches used both of their time-outs.

Now you hear the complaint that this system would open a Pandora's box. Baloney. If the supreme ref saw another infraction while he was looking at the monitor, forget it, he can only rule on the merits of the *original* appeal. A coach gets only one shot, and that's on the original call. If the appeals ref sees eight other guys holding, too bad, he has to ignore it.

Finally, *boo on the overtime rule in football.*

For one team to win the flip in overtime, receive the kickoff, get a good runback, move 40 yards, kick a field goal to win the game, and the other team hasn't even touched the ball—this is wrong. It would be like a tie game in baseball after nine innings: The visiting team scores in the top of the tenth and the game's over, with the home team never coming to bat. That's wrong.

Both teams should have the ball at least one time. After that, they're on their own.

If you take the opening kickoff in overtime and score, then you have to kick off to me until I either score or lose the ball. If I do score and tie the game, then I kick off to you. If you score again, the game's over. True, you had the ball twice and I only had it once. But at least we both had the ball—and a chance to score, which is not the case now.

9

Predictions and Guarantees

If you have ever seen my pro picks on Friday night during football season, you know what they're like. Not mediocre, not poor, but *terrible*. Usually, you can take my picks and go the opposite way. It's a kind of joke, actually.

In the fall of 1981, though, I had a very good year. Maybe my only good year. The Jets were a two-point favorite over the Dolphins. ''Wrong,'' I said. ''The *Jets* will win by only one point, 21–20. Take Miami and the points.'' Final score: Jets 16, Dolphins 15. Now it's the last game of the season, Giants versus the Cowboys. Dallas is a four-point favorite. ''Wrong,'' I said. ''The Giants will win by three, 17–14. Take the Giants and the points.'' Final score: Giants 13, Cowboys 10. The two biggest games of the year in New York, I got both point spreads right on the nose. I'm on a cloud, right? I mean, these have to be the greatest picks in my life.

You'd never know it.

The Saturday night after the Giants game, my wife and I go to Vivolo's restaurant on the Upper East Side. We're eating our soup, just minding our business, when this guy yells out. ''Hey, Warner, when ya' goin' to give us a winner?'' he says. ''Ya' know a guy can go broke listenin' to your stuff.'' I just laughed. Waved my hand. What's the use of explaining? What he said might have been true some other year. But he picked the wrong year and certainly the wrong week.

The point is, if you are a sportscaster, have fun on the air with your picks. Don't take it too seriously. Don't be afraid to be wrong.

I do the picks for fun. I'll be wrong or I'll be right. It's pure entertainment.

I'll never forget the January 1983 Super Bowl game. Washington and Miami. Miami is a 2½- to 3-point favorite. However, I liked Washington. So I went on the air, both locally in New York on WCBS-TV and nationally on the *CBS Morning News* and picked the Redskins, 20–17. Well, as you know, the Redskins won 27–17. Naturally I was pleased with the outcome. I was only 7 points off the actual score. But I have to tell you something. During the game I actually became greedy. Selecting the right team all of a sudden wasn't enough for me. I wanted to hit the score right on the nose. With two minutes to go in the game, it *was* 20–17 Redskins, *my* score, but the Skins were driving. Suddenly, it appears that fullback John Riggens fumbles and the ball is recovered by Miami at the Miami 15. I jump out of my seat at home, hollerin', "All right, way to go!" My wife says, "What's the matter with you, I thought you picked the Redskins?" I say, "I did, but I don't want 'em to score *again*. I've got the score right on the nose."

Instead of realizing for the moment that if the Skins fumble and lose the ball Miami could at least tie the game 20–20, or even win the game, I miss everything. All I see is that I've got a shot at picking the exact score of the biggest game of the year on national TV. Well, it was all academic, of course, because the referee ruled that Riggens's knee had touched the ground before he lost the ball and there was no fumble. So, on third down, Joe Theisman hits Charley Brown for the touchdown and suddenly it's no longer my 20–17 score—it's 27–17. What a letdown! The point is, you gotta have fun with your picks and can't get carried away.

Same thing with my predictions. Probably one of the best I made was the first Ali-Frazier fight. March 8, 1971, Madison Square Garden. Ali had recently returned from his exile. Both fighters were undefeated. Most people picked Ali. I went on Channel 9 and said,

"Folks, I predict Joe Frazier will defeat Ali in a fifteen-round decision. No question about it. Frazier by decision."

When you predict, obviously it's fun because you run the risk of looking bad. You want to be right, of course, but it's not curtains if you aren't. I saw the fight on closed-circuit TV at the Washington Hilton Hotel. I'll never forget it. Frazier knocks Ali down in the fifteenth round and I start yelling, "Get up! Get up, you bum! Get up!" I wanted Frazier to win by decision, not by knockout. I remember the guy in front of me turned around, looked at me, and said, "Ali's not a bum. How can you call him a bum?" Of course he wasn't. No way. I just wanted to be right. As it happened, I scored the fight the way I used to do at home in front of the radio. I had it right on the nose. The same way referee Arthur Mercante scored it. Eight rounds Frazier, six rounds Ali, one even. Decision Frazier. Greatest fight of the decade as far as I was concerned.

I'll tell you when I wasn't right on a prediction: October 1970. Fourth game of the season, Lions against the Redskins, RFK Stadium. The Lions are 3–0, the Redskins 1–2. I go on the air Friday night and hold up a card saying, "Lions, 31–10." You know who won? The Redskins. You know the score? 31–10. Bad, man. Not only was I wrong, but I was wrong by exactly the same score! I was in my seat near the 50-yard line, and the fans booed me the entire second half.

One thing I am serious about are guarantees. You can never be wrong on a guarantee or it would be all over. If I make a prediction and I'm wrong, okay, I'll razz myself. I'll go on the air and bomb myself. You have to do this to show people you're willing to be a good sport about it. But when you guarantee something, man, this is your word. It's binding. You absolutely must be sure. No excuses permitted.

Every once in a while, I get a strange feeling inside. It's like I feel something so deeply, I *know* it will happen. It's automatic. Guaranteed. This feeling doesn't occur often. But when it does, it's the most natural thing in the world to make the guarantee. It's reason, but it goes beyond reason. When you try to picture the guaranteed outcome going the other way, it doesn't work. All I can tell you is it's a unique sensation. You have no doubt—no doubt whatsoever.

Only two times in twenty-two years on the air have I felt things so strongly that I've guaranteed something. The first was a Washington Redskins at Dallas Cowboys game in December 1979. A month before, the Redskins had beaten the Cowboys in Washington. I saved this game for the end of my pro picks Friday night. "Folks, I guarantee Dallas will beat Washington for this reason: I have seen every Cowboys-Redskins game since Dallas came into the league in 1960, and never have the Redskins beaten the Cowboys twice in the same regular season. I guarantee. Cowboys over the Redskins."

The Giants were on television in New York. As soon as the Giants game ended, CBS cut to Dallas. Five minutes to go, Redskins ahead, 34–21. Dallas looks dead. My guarantee looks dead. Even Tom Landry looks sterner than usual.

Now it's down to two minutes, twenty seconds. Cowboys get the ball, Roger Staubach throws to Ron Springs—*touchdown!* It's 34–28 with the extra point. Cowboy defense stops the Redskins cold, Staubach gets the ball, passes to Tony Hill—*touchdown!* It's tied at 34. Rafael Septien kicks the extra point, the Redskins can't do a thing in the final thirty-nine seconds, and the Cowboys win, 35–34. What a game! The Redskins are out of the playoffs, Staubach is a hero again, and my first guarantee comes out. I'm saved! Unbelievable how this happened. I have to admit I had my doubts with two minutes to go. But I also must say that two days earlier I *knew*—as sure as I was sitting there—that the Cowboys would win.

The other time I guaranteed was July 1981, the light-heavyweight championship fight between Michael Spinks and Eddie Mustafa Muhammad. Mustafa was the champ. Spinks had been living in the shadow of his brother Leon. All of a sudden, I get this incredible feeling. Totally logical. Absolutely clear. Kind of like a preview in my mind. I go on the air and say, "Folks, I will guarantee—*guarantee without question*—that Michael Spinks will beat Eddie Mustafa Muhammad and win the light-heavyweight championship of the world. People don't realize how good Spinks is because his brother gets all the publicity. He's so much better than Leon it's not even close. *GUARANTEED!* Spinks will win."

I turn on the set and Spinks, the first eight rounds, he's not doing beans. I've never seen him like this. He's hardly landing a punch. My wife is watching with me. "This is bad, man," I tell her. "What am I gonna do if it stays like this?" Fortunately, Spinks finally comes on, knocks Mustafa down in the thirteenth round, and wins a unanimous decision. What I learned later was this: Spinks figured Mustafa was a slow starter, so he paced himself the first eight rounds. If I'd known that, I wouldn't have given a guarantee. You're taking a chance when you do that.

So I've made only two guarantees. Now it's possible I'll never guarantee again, because I may never have that feeling again. But I've come close. Before the second Sugar Ray Leonard–Roberto Duran fight—the *no mas, no mas* fight in which Duran gave up—I said that without question, Leonard will beat Duran. I figured that Leonard, even while fighting Duran's fight the first time, almost beat him. It was a stupid fight by Leonard, but he lost by a total of only four points from three judges. So I said this time he's going to fight his own fight and he's going to win, no question about it. I made it a prediction, not a guarantee.

It all goes back to show business. Roy Campanella used to say that to succeed in baseball, you need a little bit of the boy in you. Well, to succeed as a sportscaster, you need a little bit of the theater in you. I could do the sportscasts straight—but that's not what people expect of me. They expect humor and entertainment from me, and that's what I give 'em. Pro picks, predictions, guarantees—everything to liven things up.

I get letters from some viewers. "Hey, you're not paid for your opinion. Just give us the scores." I write them back. "On the contrary, sir," I say, "I *am* paid for my opinions and not giving the scores. If you want the scores, pick up the newspaper or dial Sportsphone. A mannequin can give the scores."

I learned to stop rolling the scores about five years ago when it became easier to get videotape of games off the satellite. "Let's go to the videotape!" I said. BOOM! No more scores unless it's the local team or a game everybody wants to know about—Yankee scores, Met scores in New York, and perhaps the team that's closest to the division title if it's August or September. But the Reds-Padres score? Minnesota against Seattle? Come on, who cares in New York? I keep saying you've got to aim for the average guy in the audience.

Sometimes I'll get phone calls. Guy calls up and wants to know why I don't give the cricket scores. "Big audience out here for cricket," he says. You know what? If I gave cricket scores, I'd probably have three more shows and then I'd be off the air. *"In other action tonight, Lancastershire beat Derby, 8–1, in the All-England Lawn and Cricket League."* Come on, gimme a break!

Other people call up. "Where's the surfboard results? Lots of interest out here in surfboard action."

"Where's the bicycle racing results?"

"How come you don't give bocci results, marble results, the roller skating championships?"

These are serious calls. I got one last year from a viewer who wondered why I didn't give the story about the New England Sharks folding.

"Uh, sir, who are the New England Sharks?"

"Come on, Warner, you don't know who the New England Sharks are? They're in the Cape Cod Conference of the Atlantic Seaboard Soccer League!"

"Oh. I'm sorry I missed that story."

Are you kidding? Who wants to know about the New England Sharks, unless you live in New England?

Let me give you my theory on videotape. Some people say, why not show more interviews and fewer highlights? The answer is easy. If it's a choice between the interview or the action, 99 out of 100 people on the street would say, "Gimme the action." Now that the technology is there, you can bring in games from all over the country. You've got to show people the action. You've got to give them games they can't see at home.

Look, these are just my opinions and my rules. Maybe they don't apply for everybody. If a young guy's coming up and he doesn't want to shout "Swish!" and "Boom!", then let him do it straight. Maybe he has a different approach, and lots of highlights wouldn't work for him. But too many guys interview somebody just to show they left the studio and went out on the street. They'll interview somebody just to show they're working. Who cares? If Ali or Wilt Chamberlain or Mantle or Namath is in town, hey, interview the guy. Have him on the show. If he's a big name, by all means. I've done long interviews with Joe DiMaggio and Leo Durocher, using two-minute segments each night for two weeks. But you're gonna interview Joe Hommizah, pole vault coach at Bogus High? Forget it, man. Show the action.

To me, the most important things are to be upbeat, to be a real person, and to make the audience feel at ease with you. Talk about the same things you would at a bar. Crack jokes, poke fun. Ask the questions the fans would ask. Nobody wants to know what Darryl Dawkins thinks of antitrust. They want to know how he felt when he broke the two backboards. If you're putting on airs, the fans will find you out. I want them to feel like I'm coming out of the set, filling up the living room and saying hello.

The truth is, there can't be bad moods in this business. People don't let other sourpusses into their homes, why should they let you in? They have enough troubles of their own. They're turning you on for relief. So as soon as the camera comes on, that's it. Fifteen years in television, it's automatic. The light comes on—BOOM!—you forget about your personal life.

One thing about television: I would feel out of place now if I didn't wear a tie. There was a short period in Washington when I wore a sport shirt open at the neck with my jacket. I figured it looked pretty good. Let the news guys wear the ties. One night I came home and my wife said, "Warner, about that shirt . . . No good."

"Whaddya mean, no good?"

"Not that it doesn't look nice, but have you ever seen Johnny Carson come on without a tie?"

"What does that have to do with it?"

"Well, he's coming into a person's home, and he's showing respect."

I have to thank my wife for this one. She was right. I've never gone on the air since without a tie. It's a matter of simple courtesy.

From time to time, I've also had to change my ways on my weight and height. The weight was the worst part. I'll never forget my first awareness of being fat: 1970. I'd been on television for a year. Television makes you look ten pounds heavier than you are anyway. Plus I had put on another ten to fifteen pounds myself. On radio, who cares? Nobody sees you. But on TV, it's a different story. I had to sweat twenty pounds off to 145. Then two years ago I had to go on a tuna fish and melon diet. I'd let fifteen pounds creep back on. I'd see my face getting fuller. I'd say, "C'mon, man, who is that guy? He can't be me."

The second thing I had to do was make myself look taller. I'm 5 feet 6 when I'm walking on my tiptoes. People think I'm a giant when they don't know me. It never fails. First reaction is always like somebody has been cheated. "Hey," they say, "I thought you were a big guy. You're a little fella, you're not tall." I usually answer by saying, "I *am* taller on TV."

Anyway, my being short was never a deterrent. Never had problems playing sports. Got along fine with girls. But after I was on television about a year, a friend of mine came up to me. "Warner, I hate to tell you this, but you know when you're on TV? It looks like you're down in a hole."

I went into the studio, looked at the videotapes, and it really did look like I was in a hole. It looked like I was trying to climb out onto the desk but couldn't make it. Sort of slumped over and going down. So, ever since, I've put extra cushions on the chair just before air time.

Sometimes being short helps. It was 1975. I was still in Washington. Instead of doing an interview behind the desk I was standing next to André the Giant, the wrestler. He's 7 feet 4, which meant I was a little taller than his belt. He's also 444 pounds. Anyway, I asked him a number of questions about king-size beds on the road and what he ate as a kid in France. But the best material we saved for the end. When we came back from the last commercial, I shook his hand. Routine goodbye. But while I'm saying so long to the audience, André puts his hand under my backside and pops me up onto his shoulder. It was like the palm of his hand was a scale. One hand—BOOM!—I'm perched on his left shoulder. Fastest lift you ever saw. It's like I'm an ornament up there. We start laughing and waving. "So long, folks! See ya later!" The tape is so popular I play it back once a year.

There are several people I should thank for helping me do all right in television—a few sportscasters and a couple of newspaper guys. They probably don't realize this, but I studied how they talked or how they wrote things. It was like going to school. Not that I stole from them. I would just see something they did and say, "Hey, I like that. That's what I would like to do if I ever get on television."

I always watched the Baltimore sportscasters. There were two guys in particular, Vince Bagli and Joe Crogan. They both had one thing in common: *They talked the sports*. This was over twenty years ago. They were unique. While other guys read the sports, Bagli and Crogan talked the sports. They spoke in a conversational manner, like you were with them in a diner or something. That's where I picked up my ad lib style. I said, "Wow! Look at those guys!" To this day I don't use the TelePrompTer or read copy. I use notes or say what comes to mind.

Two other announcers who helped me on play-by-play were Ray Scott and Chuck Thompson. I listened to both guys for years and eventually worked with Scott. Most announcers back then gave you a kind of radio call even if they were on television. The more words the better. Didn't matter if you could see what they were telling you. Scott and Thompson were rarities in that they adjusted their television announcing to the camera. They knew you didn't need to describe everything if the camera showed it. Say it was first down and Paul Hornung of the Packers gained 5 yards off tackle. As the play was happening, Scott would go, "Hornung . . . five yards . . . stop made by Lilly." Thompson would do the same thing in baseball. Say Mantle flied out to the Orioles' Paul Blair in center. Thompson would go, "Blair should have it . . . two out." To me, this was great. You could see that Mantle hit the ball and that the ball was going to center. Why announce it?

Then there were two columnists, Morris Siegel of the *Washington Star* and Shirley Povich of the *Washington Post*. Siegel was everywhere. Besides the newspaper, he was at Channel 4, Channel 7, and Channel 9 in Washington. The thing I learned was that he always put humor into his sportscast. It made things entertaining. He'd give his opinion and then he'd crack jokes. "Let's go to the scoreboard," he'd say. "Let's see here, Haig and Haig, 81, Johnny Walker, 80."

Povich was one of the greatest writers I ever read. I think that reading him for twenty-five years helped my content. It influenced what I said on the air and taught me to look for new points to bring out. Plus he had an unusual way of saying things. He would use an understatement to get his point across. I remember once he was writing about the 1948 Senators, a seventh-place team. "Well," he said, "they can't field. But they can't hit, either." Then he would start off stories like this: "Jim Brown, in one 90-yard run yesterday, taught George Preston Marshall the wisdom of being color blind." No way I could come up with lines like that. But what Povich did was sharpen my taste for tongue-in-cheek expressions.

10

Suggestions for TV

You can't force happy talk.

In 1970, at Channel 9, Max Robinson, Gordon Peterson, and I started in Washington what is referred to as happy talk. We liked each other. We had a natural rapport. We'd kid around, but nothing was ever rehearsed. To me, that's the key right there. Nothing was forced. It's forced when the anchorman thinks he has to respond to everything the weather guy or sports guy says, no good. Come on, you don't have to make chit-chat if it isn't natural. Viewers won't buy it. I've always worked better when the weatherman and the anchorman respond, when the cameramen start laughing right in the middle of my material. It's like having a live audience.

No sideline interviews!

In my opinion, reporters have no right to be on the field during a game. Get the reporters out of there. It's intruding. You can't interview a player or a coach during the game and expect his mind to be on the action. It would be like during a war, a TV reporter runs up to a soldier on the battlefield and says, ''Excuse me, corporal, how many grenades have you dodged today?'' Come on, the guy's in a war. Leave him alone. Let's say a lawyer is examining a witness. Do you run up and say, ''Excuse me, counsel, was the defendant telling the truth when she answered that last question?''

One of the things I dislike most is the shot of the player saying

"Hi, Mom!" Not only is it overused, it takes the guy's mind off the game for that moment. He should be concentrating on the game, not mugging for television. He owes it to his team. But it's not the player who's at fault here. The blame rests on television. After all, it isn't the player who's distracting the camera.

I saw a boxing match last year on national TV. I couldn't believe it. The TV guy was in the ring interviewing the fighters *before* the decision. That's wrong. It's intruding. At least wait till after the decision. You know where this is going to end? Someday soon there's going to be a basketball game and some guy is going to be at the foul line when a reporter sticks a mike in his face. "Now look, you're going to shoot these two foul shots. You aiming for the front of the rim or the back of the rim?" Come on! Get him off!

One more thing along the same line. If I were the head of a professional sport, I would make it illegal for active coaches or players to have shows on television during their season. I don't care what people say. When a coach or player knows he's later going to have to be on television and explain why he made his decision, it's going to affect his thinking in the game.

The box shot.

One shot that bugs me in TV sports coverage is the small box in the corner of the screen. It seems that every sports producer thinks he has to show a split screen with a box in the corner. The box will show a player's mother, a fighter's wife, a runner standing at third, a coach, or a crowd reaction—while the action is still going on the rest of the field.

Come on, it's distracting. When you go to a game you don't see a box out of the corner of your right eye. You are concentrating on the action in front of you.

I've seen plays missed because of the box. Cut out the box!

Special reports!

Every local TV station in the country runs what they call specials on the nightly news in February, May, and November. These are the big rating months, and are crucial because they determine sales rates for the entire year. Thinking that viewers love specials, station executives go crazy putting them on. They'll run three minutes, four minutes, sometimes five minutes a night. They'll sometimes last one or two weeks. "And now for our continuing look into 'Fraud in the Parking Meter System: Are Meter Maids on the Take?' "

The other nine months of the year they don't emphasize specials. They just act normal. But every February, May, and November, they go wild. "Fraud in the Hat Business" . . . "The Pothole Problem in Queens" . . . "The High Cost of Getting Sick." This has never made any sense to me. I think these specials chase away the viewers. No way you can hold their attention that long. They want to see what you do best the other nine months. That's why they tuned you in. Don't change just because it's a rating period.

It's like having a certain personality nine months of the year and then acting different the other three months just because important people are now watching. That's not right. The regular viewers have been with you for nine months. They like you because you're the way you are. Why change?

I'm convinced that as soon as one station in a market stops putting on specials and is successful, all the other stations will follow. Television is a copy medium.

Long convention and election coverage.

This is one of my network opinions. Except for politicians, I can't believe anyone wants to sit in front of a television set from 7 to 11 p.m. and watch four hours of gavel to gavel convention and election coverage. It's too repetitious. That's why the independent stations that show movies during the conventions and elections kill the network stations. This happened in New York in 1980. One of the independents ran *Casablanca* and bombed the three owned-and-operated stations. Come on, nobody wants to see gavel to gavel. But because one station carries it, the others do. Like I said, it's a copycat business.

Too many news teases!

A tease is when the station, in fear of losing you when it goes to a commercial, says, "Coming up, Joe Homitz and his report on jukeboxes" and they show videotape. This is supposed to hold your interest. I say there are too many teases. Plus, teases are sometimes a trick. The station comes back from commercial and you don't immediately see the story. The jukebox story could even be after the *next* commercial.

All local television is tease crazy, even though it uses up valuable news time. I get 4 minutes out of 22½ minutes on the 11 o'clock news. It's better than one-sixth of the show, so I can't complain. But how about the other news reporters? They could use the extra time. You could save some valuable TV news time by shortening, or even doing away with, some of the news teases.

Telephone interviews on television.

Ever see an anchorman or sportsman interviewing somebody on the telephone? Come on, give us a break! This is television, not radio. To sit and watch an anchorman or sports guy look into a camera with a telephone in his hand, interviewing somebody, is bad TV—as I said, it's radio, not TV.

11

New York, New York!

Living in Washington, I never realized just how important sports could be to a New Yorker. That is, until October 3, 1950. I was almost 13 years old.

I'm at home right after school watching a national game on television. Brooklyn Dodgers versus New York Giants. Final inning of the final game for the National League playoffs. The Dodgers are ahead, 4–2, last of the ninth, but as everyone knows, the Giants win, 5–4, on Bobby Thomson's three-run homer.

I was watching the game with one of my friends, Bobby Lippman, who had just moved to Washington from Brooklyn. As soon as Thomson hit the home run, he threw his school books down on my floor and started screaming, "Oh, my," he yells, "this can't be happening! How could you do this to me?" Then he ran out of my house and slammed the door. It was like a bomb had hit. I sat there, dumbfounded.

"This is amazing," I said to myself. "What does he care if the Dodgers lost to the Giants? It's only a game. I mean, *really*. What's this big deal about New York and Brooklyn?" As I later realized, it was a big deal, far and away the biggest in Bobby Lippman's and a lot of other people's lives. You've got to realize the power of New York City. He had grown up his whole life in Brooklyn and his Dodgers lost to the Giants! He slammed my door so hard I thought it was going to come off the hinges. He was holding his head, hollering. But to me, who cared about New York? The Senators weren't that big. Why should anybody get carried away like that, just because New York had beaten Brooklyn?

Of course, you later get indoctrinated. New York is where the networks are. It's where everything happens. You're taught that. If you want to be number one, you have to go to the network or go to New York. You have to get with the program.

This is the way it was in my case. I was the sportscaster on Channel 9 and I was happy doing what I was doing. The people in Washington liked my work. But when I got a phone call from the president of ABC Sports, I couldn't resist. Looking back, I'm glad I went to the network. I would do it the same way again. Otherwise, how would I ever know?

The first call from the president of ABC Sports was exciting. I got it in the summer of 1974. Right out of the blue.

"Hello, I'd like to speak to Warner Wolf, please."

"Speaking."

"You don't know me, but I'm the president of ABC Sports in New York. Warner, we've been watching your work. What's your contract situation down there? Have you ever thought of being on national television?"

Are you kidding? *National* television? The network? Man, I was ready. I liked Washington, it was my home town and all, but I always figured you have to grab the opportunity when it arises. For five years I had said no to job offers on local stations. New York, Atlanta, Detroit, Chicago, and Los Angeles. But this was *network*. My contract at Channel 9 was paying me $85,000 a year. It had a few more years to run. He said I could have $150,000 a year. Even though New York was expensive to live in, that kind of money would still go a long way. Plus I figured I could eventually keep a permanent home in Washington. Keith Jackson, Chris Schenkel, and Jim McKay lived out of town and worked in New York, why couldn't I?

He told me to catch the next morning's shuttle up to New York. I flew up with my lawyer, Ivan Shefferman, and by 11 a.m. I was in his office on the twenty-fourth floor of the ABC Building at 54th and Sixth Avenue.

We sit down on a sofa and he tells me how much ABC likes my work. He says they like personalities at ABC. He starts talking to me about a deal, contingent on Channel 9 being willing to release me from my contract. I would sign with ABC that fall. He said I'd be a natural at ABC. He said they'd have me doing just about everything, including *Wide World of Sports,* and also reminded me that ABC had the 1976 summer and winter Olympics. There also was a clause that I had to do sportscasts on WABC–Channel 7, the ABC owned-and-operated station in New York, if and when my network schedule permitted.

I told him I'd get back to him. But back in Washington, the reaction was understandable. No way. I had 2½ years to go on my contract and Channel 9 would not let me out of it. Instead, they gave me the play-by-play of the Bullets and the color commentary on the Capitals' telecasts that winter, which made me happy.

One year goes by. Everybody's happy at Channel 9. Finally the phone rings, and it's that voice from New York again.

"Hello, Warner? This is the president of ABC Sports. Why don't you see if they'll let you out of your contract *now*? We'd still like to have you." Well, believe it or not, one of my attorneys, Tom Powers, of Washington, D.C., found a loophole in my contract that permitted me to leave WTOP earlier than expected. Amicable agreement. No grudges, no backbiting. All clean on both sides. ABC would still have me in time for the winter Olympics in 1976. And even though I was working for ABC on the weekends, I would stay at Channel 9 Monday through Friday nights till March 1976. This was an extremely unusual deal, since Channel 9 was a CBS affiliate.

Prior to my agreement with ABC Sports was the irony that as soon as word got around to CBS and NBC that ABC wanted me, they started making offers too. That's the way the networks work. If one guy wants you, they all want you. That was an incredible summer for me in 1975. As it turned out, the other two networks actually offered slightly more than ABC. They dropped hints that I'd be able to do pro football, boxing, and baseball. But ABC made the first offer and showed the most interest so I felt I owed them an allegiance. After I got permission from Channel 9, I called ABC back and said, "It's a deal."

I worked for ABC network from September 1975 to March 6, 1978. Although I will never go down in ABC sports history as one of their great highlights of all time, it *was* one of the most interesting $2^1/_2$ year periods I ever spent in broadcasting. In 1977, when I went back to local television in New York full time on WABC–TV and things worked out, I was able to appreciate success all the more. Success is only fully appreciated after you've been a failure.

The interesting thing is that while going to the ABC network turned out to be a mistake, I'm glad I did it. It's the only way you learn. Not only did I see how the networks operate, I found out how to deal with a few problems that almost everybody in television runs into. I have a general theory about problems. You confront them. Directly. You control them before they control you.

First, going to the network and being in New York taught me how to deal with fame. Look, don't get me wrong. You want fame. It's human. The first time I was on television in Washington, I went into a restaurant the next day and looked around to see if anyone recognized me. Nobody did. Nothing wrong with that. You want the pulse. If they don't know who you are, you're nothing in this business. But you have to be able to manage fame. Otherwise it will eat you up.

The truth is it took me a while to learn how to handle fame. Radio doesn't prepare you for it. You can be a famous radio personality and walk down the street and nobody will know it's you. It's a rarity that someone comes up and says, "Wait a minute. I recognize your voice. Aren't you Sammy What's-your-name?" When you get on television, they come up constantly. "Hey, Warner, let's go to the videotape! Come on, Warner, gimme a break!" Plus they expect you to be exactly the way you are on TV. They want to talk sports. They want you to confirm their opinion that George Steinbrenner, say, deserves the Boo of the Week.

Once Sue and I went to the Shoreham Hotel in Washington, D.C., for a function and this viewer comes up. He's excited to see me. Almost bouncy-like. "Well, Warner, how do you think the

Skins will do this year? Another Super Bowl trip?'' He expected me to come across with my on-the-air personality. Instead, it was my off-the-air personality, certainly more low-key than my *on*-the-air personality. I mean does Frank Sinatra go around singing in public when he's not on stage? No. It's just that you're different off the air. Well, the guy looked totally, absolutely surprised. ''What's the matter?'' he said. ''Something wrong?'' After we went inside, this guy was still on my mind. ''Man, why's he so excited?'' I said to Sue. ''What does he expect? A show right here? I'm off the air.''

My wife taught me a valuable lesson. ''Warner,'' she said, ''what you don't understand is all he sees is the Warner Wolf on television. He sees this high-pitched performer who's ready to go. He thinks that's the way you always are. You have to be a little more outgoing. Be glad he came up to you.''

Ever since that day I try to smile or joke or talk sports with everyone. Come on, this is the way it has to be. You can't give them this deadpan stuff. Without the fans, you're not on the air. You're zero. Be glad they're coming up. That's the only reason you're on—because they like you.

Another lesson I learned occurred in May 1976. My wife and I were invited to go to LA for an ABC affiliates meeting. All the big ABC stars were there—Jaclyn Smith and Kate Jackson, of *Charlie's Angels,* Captain and Tenille, Starsky and Hutch, Charo, the late Paul Linde, and Gabe Kaplan, of *Welcome Back, Kotter*. But without question, two people stood out in my mind above all the rest. One was Henry Winkler, the ''Fonz.'' Winkler introduced himself to my two daughters, and later mailed them ''Fonz'' T-shirts. He was great and unaffected.

The other person was veteran movie actor Robert Stack. Stack (Elliot Ness) came up and introduced himself to Sue and me and started a conversation. All I could think of was, here is a room full of stars and two of the most humble people were two of the biggest—Winkler, who was number one in the country at the time, and Stack, who had made movies for forty years with some of the greatest stars in Hollywood. What a great lesson.

In New York you really know you've made it when they name

a sandwich after you. In 1980, the Stars' Deli, 52nd and Lexington, adds to their menu the *Warner Wolf sandwich*: three-decker with hot brisket of beef, chopped liver, sweet red pepper, and special dressing. All for $5.95.

A thought on autographs. If you have time to stand and sign, great. But if you're headed somewhere, keep moving. Sign in motion. I learned this four years ago. I was leaving WABC's studio on West 66th Street. I was on my way home to pick up my daughter for a doctor's appointment. I mean, I had to get home. I had to pick her up at 3:30 sharp or she'd be late.

I come out of the studio and there happen to be twenty-five people waiting for the soap opera stars across the street. Suddenly they spot me and they're shouting for me to sign. You can't say no because then you're a villain. They don't want to hear, "Sorry, I can't sign, gotta pick up my daughter for her doctor's appointment." That's a boo, man. It's like, "C'mon, how do we know he's not making that up? Maybe he just doesn't want to sign." So, you walk and sign. Now a lot of people want your autograph but not *that* bad. They won't follow you. You see, these twenty-five people at the studio really were waiting for a soap opera star. When they saw me, it was like, "Well, as long as we're here, let's get this guy, too." Those who really wanted my autograph walked with me. Those who didn't, stopped.

So you learn to deal with it. The thing I've never been able to understand is how some celebrities go out and say, "Gee, I was interrupted eating my spaghetti by eight people." I've always said if you don't want the recognition, then don't eat out. Get room service. Forget being interrupted. You've got to accept the public because the public makes you. That's the price you pay. Get that through your head. You're not like everybody else. You're recognizable. In essence, it's the people on the street who are really paying your salary. Because if those people don't watch you, you're a zero.

Fame is all temporary anyway. The key is to make the most of it so when the day comes when you don't have fame or success, you're taken care of.

Now one thing all performers must deal with at one time or another is nervousness. Don't ever let anybody tell you they're not nervous when they try something new. It's the most natural thing in the world. *Monday Night Baseball.* The Olympics. The time I started my new half-hour show in New York on Tuesday nights. Sure, you're nervous. Absolutely. The thing that makes you nervous is the fear of failure. You're scared you won't look good. You start talking to yourself before you go on. You try to memorize things because maybe you'll draw a blank when the camera goes on. Once you start talking, the nervousness should go away. Now if it doesn't go away, you've got some problems. Maybe you'd better not be in the business. You can't do a whole sportscast and be nervous.

As a performer, you must also learn how to handle criticism. I used to take some razzing in Washington, but it was nothing compared to New York. The thing is, you have to form a certain shell. You'll never please everybody, you'd better get that straight from the start. People are going to write about you in this business. By forming a shell you have to get to the point where you realize it's not all five hundred people on the newspaper or magazine who are against you. It's only that one person writing the column.

Does what they say hurt? Sure it hurts. Any performer who says, "Ahhh, critics don't bother me," isn't telling the truth. But you forget about it the next day. If it was a cheap shot, you may wonder why the guy took it. But then it's gone. If it was valid criticism, you think about it and maybe it helps you. But you move on. Plus I also look at it this way when a piece comes out that knocks me: I think how glad I am to be in this country, where a guy can write what he wants. If that same writer were in Russia writing for *Pravda,* he could only write what the government wanted him to write. Here he's free to write practically anything he wants.

Another point is, sports fans are very loyal. If they don't like you, the greatest write-up in the world won't change their minds. They're still not going to like you. On the other hand, if they like you and a guy bombs you in the paper, they'll still like you. It's when they *stop* writing about you that you have a problem. It doesn't matter what they say, as long as they spell your name right. There are only two people you have to please in this business: the fans and your boss.

Marvin Kittman of *Newsday* bombed me when I first came to New York. Absolutely killed me. But people wrote in to me to say, "Don't worry what he says, just hang in there. We like you." I didn't think anything more of it. About a month after his article, I got a huge envelope in the mail with about five hundred letters in it. From Kittman. Almost all the letters were from people bombing *him* for bombing me. Plus there was a note on *Newsday* stationery. "I stand corrected," it said. "Best regards, Marvin Kittman." Wasn't that nice? He was a man about it. It goes to show that not all critics are out to get you.

Then there was Morris Siegel, whom I spoke of earlier. He criticized me for eleven years in Washington. He once referred to me as a "bushy haired interrogator." Another time I was the "bubble gum whiz kid." He used to kill me. And at times it hurt. But what he did made me famous. He helped put me on the map because he would constantly mention my name. "As Warner Wolf, the bushy haired interrogator, would say . . ." Sure the razzing bothered me. But in a way, it was a compliment. In the summer many people in Washington go to Rehoboth Beach, Delaware, for vacation. One time I went to the beach and had dinner with him. Our kids played on the beach together. I get back to Washington and he writes, "Warner Wolf has signed a long-term television contract. He bought three TVs and got a warranty." Anything to razz me, see? But it was great. That was Morris Siegel's way.

Finally somebody asked me on the air, "Do you mind Morrie Siegel writing bad about you?" I said, "No, not as long as he spells my name right." Siegel must have been listening. The next week he writes, "*Warren* Wolf, the bubble gum whiz kid . . ."

Besides press criticism, you also can get pressure from the sports leagues when you come to New York. They're all based in New York, so they see your stuff on the local news.

I remember one time, the Colts are playing the Patriots, a Sunday afternoon, late 1977. The game has an effect on who gets into the playoffs. Bert Jones of the Colts takes the snap from center and—BOOM!—the Patriots tee off on him. He fumbles the ball and the

Patriots recover. But, hold everything! It wasn't a fumble, says the referee. "Jones was down *before* he fumbled. Dead ball! Colts retain possession!"

Unbelievable call. I mean, it didn't even look close. The replay seemed to prove he fumbled before the whistle blew.

Now back then the NFL had a rule that network affiliates could not use clips of the TV games until twenty-four hours later. So it wasn't until 6 p.m. Monday that anybody could show the play. I come into the studio for my 11 o'clock show and find out that the 6 o'clock guy didn't use the clips. I go to the producer of the early news and ask what happened.

"Oh, you know what?" he says. "We got a call from this guy from the NFL. He said we weren't allowed to put on the highlights."

"Weren't allowed?" I said. "Come on, Channel Two used 'em at six o'clock. Channel Four used 'em. No way two other stations can use 'em and we can't."

That Monday night our late news was on around midnight because we had to wait for *Monday Night Football* to be over. I come on during a station break while the game is in progress—it must have been about 10:45—and say, "I'll be here after the game and we'll have the fumble that wasn't a fumble!"

BOOM! No sooner do I get off the air than my phone rings. It's the guy from the NFL.

"Warner," he says, "you can't use these highlights. We have an embargo on them."

I say, "Let me tell you something. No way in the world you can tell me we can't use 'em. The twenty-four hours are up, plus the other two stations used the highlights at six. No way you can block us—because that's discrimination."

"Look, I've already spoken to the other stations," he says. "They're not going to use the clips on the late news either."

"Come on, they've already used them! It doesn't matter what they do at eleven."

"Well," he says, "at least wait for a different angle. Wait a day and we'll give you another angle that shows the referee was really right."

I told him to forget waiting. If he had a different angle then and there, all right, I'd show both angles. But he was trying to censor us, see? You got to be careful. You got to use your own instincts in this business.

Another thing is, you must have patience. There were those long months when I wasn't being used on ABC Network Sports. I was going to ask for an early termination of my contract and consider returning to Washington, D.C. But my wife told me to serve out the contract as a point of principle. We did.

As far as I'm concerned, the reward for patience came in June 1979. It was about a year after I started doing both the 6 and 11 o'clock sportscasts for WABC–Channel 7. The *New York Daily News* ran a survey in which people could clip out this coupon and name their favorite sportscaster. Don't ever let sportscasters tell you they don't watch those newspaper polls. They watch them like hawks. I was new, so I was a little wary. I really didn't know what to expect. After all, the last three or four years, I hadn't been the greatest success in the history of television. But it turned out to be a plus for me. The poll came out and it was overwhelming. Something like 3–1 in my favor over the nearest competitor. I never expected it to be like that. It was the first time I realized what was happening to me in New York. Man, the biggest city in America and I was catching on.

I can remember my last 6 o'clock show at WTOP–Channel 9 in Washington: March 5, 1976. They must have gone into an old closet to come back with photos of the mid-1960s of me on radio. Fat face. Short hair. I did my sportscast, and the entire *Eyewitness News* team came onto the set to say goodbye. Frank Herzog, Maureen Bunyon, J. C. Hayward, Gordon Peterson, and Max Robinson, who went on to ABC News. They all shook my hand. I looked into the camera and said, "I never say goodbye. I just say so long."

On the 11 o'clock show that night, it was a little different. I looked into the camera and said, "You know what? Without you I'd never have been here eleven years." It was true. And I'd say the same thing now in New York. Then I gave them a smile and, as always, said, "This is Warner Wolf."

Although it was tough to leave the security and comfort of Washington, D.C., I never had second thoughts at this point. First

I remembered my father telling me how he left Washington as a young man to go on the stage in vaudeville, so it seemed like a natural move. Second, God has always blessed me with great confidence. I never think of failure.

The other beautiful thing was a farewell dinner they had for me in December 1975 at the Sheraton Park Hotel. It was a benefit with the proceeds going to the Washington Committee for Soviet Jewry. Basically, the money goes to help people who want to get out of the Soviet Union. I started getting involved with it in the early 1970s after a thought popped into my mind. One day it dawned on me that there was only one difference between me and a Jewish guy my age over in Russia: I was born here and he was born there. Otherwise, I could be in Russia, not being able to be a sportscaster because I wouldn't be allowed to say what I feel. And he'd be over here, free to say and do what he wants. It just didn't seem right.

The Soviet Jewry people have the dinner and who should they invite but George F. Will, the political analyst. The guy's terrific. Brilliant. He could run for office. His only problem is he's a Cubs fan (only kidding). They have a table with an empty chair for Andrei Sakharov, the physicist. He had just won the Nobel Peace Prize but the Russians wouldn't let him out to pick it up. Wow, what an evening! Will said the evening was festive because of me, but said it was also solemn because the next day was Human Rights Day.

I got up and said Americans have a lot to be thankful for. Man, if you don't have freedom and can't speak your piece, what do you have?

For me, the only other Soviet Jewry event that rivaled this was Solidarity Day in New York, 1979. They have Solidarity Day every April. It's an outdoor rally near the United Nations Building. You get 100,000 people marching down Fifth Avenue, down to 47th Street and over to the United Nations Plaza.

One of the things Soviet Jewry does is give bracelets for people to wear in return for donations. It's like the POW bracelets in the Vietnam War. Each bracelet has a person's name on it plus the date he or she was put in jail in the Soviet Union. You buy the bracelet and wear it until hopefully the person is released.

About six months before, I had purchased an Edward Kuznetsov bracelet. Kuznetsov had been in prison ten years for trying to leave the country—keeping in mind it was practically impossible to leave legally. On this particular day, they tied the Solidarity rally to five men who had just been released. They were Kuznetsov, Alexander Ginsburg, and three others. They flew them in from Austria and gave them seats on the platform. Their presence made it special.

I found out that Kuznetsov was released when I was at the station one night getting ready to do my sports show. The word came over the Associated Press news wire. It was an incredible feeling to know that I was wearing the bracelet of one of the men who was released.

After the march, I made my way to the platform. There's a policeman at the foot of the steps. I show the officer my bracelet and tell him I want to see Kuznetsov. Fortunately, the policeman recognizes me and says, "Go right up."

Once on the platform, I began to ask where is Edward Kuznetsov? Finally, somebody points him out. He was standing with one of the organizers off to the side. He was a short man like me, my age. Head nearly shaved, and he was wearing a gray suit that was a little too big for him, probably because of all the weight he lost in prison.

"Mr. Kuznetsov?" I said.

He looked at me and nodded. He didn't speak English. So I took off the bracelet and showed it to him. I pointed to his name. He held the bracelet up so he could see his name. Then he turned to me and clutched me. A tight embrace. We both began to cry. I remember thinking that there's no way I can understand what this guy has gone through. I also remember thinking this was the first time in my life I had ever hugged a Russian.

12

Interviewing the Greats in New York

One of the guys I'm frequently asked about is Yankee owner George Steinbrenner. As an owner, Steinbrenner is great for the fans—perhaps the best fans' owner in sports today. Whatever players the Yankees need, he goes out and buys 'em. Some people say, "Well, so what, all he does is buy players—the best team money can buy." Hey, Steinbrenner didn't make up the rules; he just takes full advantage of 'em.

But when it comes to Steinbrenner as a person, I can't agree with his style. Even though he owns the team and pays the salaries, I think it's wrong for him to ridicule and embarrass his own players, coaches, and managers in *public*. If you're going to criticize, do it in private.

I'll never forget game two of the 1980 playoffs between the Yankees and the Royals. Kansas City leads, one game to none. The score is Royals 3, Yankees 2. Top of the eighth, two outs, Willie Randolph on first. Bob Watson hits a shot into the left field corner, by Willie Wilson. Yanks third base coach Mike Ferraro, now manager of Cleveland, waves Randolph home. Wilson's relay goes over U. L. Washington's head. But George Brett backs up U. L., wheels and throws to catcher Darrell Porter, and Randolph is out at the plate. What a play! Come on, show it again, let's go to the videotape!

Kansas City goes wild. Randolph is out and so are the Yankees. Yanks lose, 3–2, and eventually lose the playoffs, three games to none.

Steinbrenner gets up from his seat and stomps out. The next day he publicly blames the loss on the coach, Ferraro, for not holding up Randolph.

I was amazed Steinbrenner would take such a position. "Look," I said on the air, "if you're down by a run in the eighth, two outs, you gotta send that guy home. What are you gonna do? Hope the next guy gets a hit with two outs? Wait till the ninth? Come on, go for it! Send him home!"

You can go to all twenty-six managers in baseball and they'd all do the same thing. Down by one, with two outs in the eighth, or ninth inning, and a guy doubles into the corner, and a good runner like Randolph is on base? Send him home! If he's out, he's out. If he's safe, the game is tied. So stop this baloney about Ferraro. The guy was doing his job exactly as it should be done.

One of my favorite guys is Billy Martin. I like Billy Martin. I've rapped him before, but as long as you're fair with Martin, he'll be fair with you.

Martin once gave me a scoop. After being fired the last time by Steinbrenner before the 1980 season, Martin became manager of the Oakland A's. Since then, of course, Martin was rehired by Steinbrenner again, the third time in the last eight years. The big question in New York that summer was whether Martin would come back in a Yankee uniform for Old Timers' Day when the A's visited Yankee Stadium. The only problem was, Martin was refusing all interviews. I called up his lawyer and friend, Doug Newton.

"Doug, is it possible I could do an interview with Billy?"

He says, "I'll call you back."

Newton calls back and says to meet Billy at his western shop on 68th and Madison at 2 p.m. Great! My crew and I go over, interview Billy, and he tells us he will show up in a Yankee uniform tomorrow for the old-timers' game. Nobody else in town has him saying on tape that he'll appear. Martin made me and Channel 2 look good, and I appreciated it.

I think Billy Martin and Earl Weaver were two of the greatest managers in the history of baseball. However, I don't think Billy will ever be 100 percent satisfied, until he owns a piece of a ball club. That way, he'll be completely in charge and will have to answer to no one.

One of the class guys I've interviewed is Joe DiMaggio. I asked DiMaggio about the night his fifty-six-game hitting streak ended—July 1941, Yankees at Cleveland. How did he feel when Ken Keltner, the Indians' third baseman, made two great stops to end the streak?

"It didn't bother me that the streak was over," DiMaggio said, "because I had another streak that was longer—sixty-one games for San Francisco in the Pacific Coast League eight years earlier. What did upset me was the way Keltner was playing me. He was practically in short left field, almost on the line. He told me later he was only trying to keep me from hitting a double, plus he knew I would never bunt. It was a close game, and he didn't want me to be on second from where I could score on a single."

Everything about DiMaggio is direct. Confident, but not cocky. He doesn't give you a preface or an index or an answer with twenty-four qualifications. Plus he was one of the most graceful players of all time. Only once did I see him do anything that was out of character. When the Dodgers' Al Gionfriddo robbed him of a homer in the 1947 World Series, he kicked the dirt in disgust.

"Joe," I said, "you had a reputation for being an unemotional player, as though you never felt the pressure . . ."

"That's not true," he said. "They said I had a poker face, but I used to laugh. I knew what was going on inside. All those years, my stomach was churning. Outside, I didn't show emotion. But inside I was plenty emotional."

"Who was the toughest pitcher for you?"

"Well," he said, "I didn't look at it that way. This may sound strange, but I wouldn't admit they were tough. I had confidence. I was supposed to hit these guys. Bob Feller was a great pitcher, but I hit him. I like to think *they* were the ones who had to face *me*, not the other way around."

Another candid guy is Ralph Branca who gave up the home run ball to Bobby Thomson in 1951. Branca was an excellent pitcher. He won twenty-one games in 1947 when he was 21 years old. Plus, not to take anything away from Thomson's homer but it really wasn't that long of a hit—a 315-foot shot that just made it into the lower left field stands. To Branca's credit, though, he never uses this as an excuse. You never hear him talking about how short the fence was.

Branca told me a little story that speaks volumes about him. After the Thomson game, he was in shock for quite a while. There are pictures of him sitting alone on his locker room stool, holding his head in his hands. Later, he got a ride home from one of his friends, who happened to be a priest. Branca got into the car and stared straight ahead. "Why me?" Branca finally asked.

"Because the Lord obviously feels that you will be strong enough to carry this," the priest replied. "Nothing happens by chance. He picked you, Ralph Branca, not somebody else. Who knows? Somebody else, this burden might wreck his life."

Man, is that some teaching? Branca is thankful for how it strengthened him. "Just tell 'em I won a few games, too," he says.

Still another guy who was down to earth was Jesse Owens, the Olympic champion. As you know, Owens won four gold medals in the 1936 Olympics, one of the most historic Olympics ever held. What you may not know is he was unaware of the furor around him.

The 1936 games were held in Berlin, just before World War II. Hitler had a box down on the field. This was going to be the Olympics in which everybody learned how superior the Aryan race was. But Owens, who was black, shot down that garbage right in front of Hitler's face.

I met Owens twice—once at WTOP in 1966 and again thirteen years later in Salisbury, North Carolina, where the National Sportscasters' and Sportswriters' Awards Dinner is held each year. Riding with Owens in the car on the way to the dinner that night, I said, "That must have been some feeling you had in the thirty-six Olympics, especially the way the world was then."

"It's funny how legends get started," Owens said. "I wasn't running for politics. I was just there to do the best job I could for Ohio State and my country. They say Hitler refused to shake my hand and snubbed me, but no one ever told me at the time. I won the four medals and I came home. The political stuff came out later."

Right after the movie *Raging Bull* came out in 1981, depicting the life story of Jake LaMotta, former middleweight champion, I decided I wanted to have him on my Tuesday night *Warner Wolf Show*. The Tuesday night show was a half-hour live show with a live audience plus a guest or two, which began in 1980 and ran for two years. It was a carryover from the same show I'd done in Washington, which was strictly with the Redskins.

As soon as I said I was thinking of having him on, people began to bad-mouth him. He must have made a lot of enemies in New York. I'd mention his name in restaurants or at shows and people would start bombing the guy.

"Ahhh, whaddya want him for? He's a dumb guy. Can't talk straight."

"LaMotta? You better have a censor handy. He'll cuss out everybody on the show."

"Geez, Warner, he's low life. You can do better than him."

Bad reaction. Lots of comments below the belt. Were they jealous of him because of the movie? Did he hurt the restaurant business in some way? I couldn't figure it. I told my wife, "Gee, hon, this guy is evil itself or a lot of people aren't giving him a chance."

You know what I discovered? A nice guy, fairly sensitive, and you *could* understand him. He said the movie was accurate on his 1947 fight against Billy Fox, the one in which the mob ordered him to take a dive if he wanted to get a shot at the middleweight title. Up to that point, LaMotta had been the number one middleweight contender, according to *Ring Magazine*, from 1943–1946, but couldn't get a title shot. Jake was a good interview. Plus he taught me that you have to find out for yourself about people. Man, if I had listened to what other people said, I would never have had him on.

LaMotta was an animal in the ring. Like Joe Frazier and Marciano and Dempsey, he had the killer instinct. They all had the kind of attitude that said, ''I gotta get that guy before he gets me.''

One guy who did not have the same killer instinct was Floyd Patterson. He was an unusual person. He said that only once in his entire career did he ever want to hurt somebody. Patterson was a peaceful guy. It bothered him that he had to beat up on people. He thought something was wrong if he had to hurt someone. However, Patterson said on my show that the only time he definitely wanted to hurt someone was in his second fight with Ingemar Johansson at the Polo Grounds in New York, 1960. The year before, Johansson had taken Patterson's heavyweight title away. Then he started making personal remarks that Patterson thought were demeaning. So Floyd was mad when he went into the ring.

In the fifth round, Patterson hit Johansson with a devastating left hook. BOOM! Johansson went down like a tree. You can look at the films. Johansson's head hits the canvas with a thud. He's lying there and his right foot begins to twitch. According to *Ring* magazine, it took eight minutes for the doctor to revive Johansson and another ten minutes before he could be helped from the ring. Patterson said he was scared that night. He said to himself, ''If this is what I have to do to earn a living, to hit a man like that, I think I want no part of it.'' He defended his title only two more times before Sonny Liston knocked him out.

Patterson told me another story that stands out as one of the greatest insights to boxing I have ever heard. In 1959, when he lost the title to Johansson in their first fight, Patterson was knocked down seven times in the third round. The thing that always intrigued me was that after the first knockdown, Patterson got up and walked *away* from Johansson. The films show the referee saying, ''Come on, come on!'' But Floyd turns his back and starts walking away. Then you see Johansson coming up from the side and knocking him down again.

Later on the show, I said, ''Floyd, what was going on there? If you had a clear enough head to get up, why didn't you cover up when you walked away?''

You know how fighters used to use the expression ''Being on Queer Street'' as a way of saying they are half-conscious in the ring? Listen to what Patterson said:

''Warner, I've watched that film over and over again. When I got up, I was so punchy that I thought *I* had knocked *Johansson* down and that *I* should walk to a neutral corner.''

Is that amazing? Here's a guy in the middle of a heavyweight championship fight and he is so far down Queer Street he thinks he just knocked the *other* guy down.

Another fighter I interviewed in New York was Gerry Cooney. He is a real-life ''Rocky,'' a Sylvester Stallone type. Same black leather jacket over a T-shirt, almost as though it's a uniform. He's a soft-spoken guy with a good sense of humor.

I had him on before his title fight with Larry Holmes, when there was still some suspicion about the quality of fighters Cooney had fought. ''Now Gerry,'' I said, ''your last three fights . . . Ken Norton, Jimmy Young, and Ron Lyle. When are you going to fight somebody your own age?'' I asked the question with a smile. I figure if you smile on a touchy question, you put them at ease while still getting your point across.

As soon as I finish, Cooney throws his hands in the air and starts shouting. ''That's it, that's it!'' he says. ''I'm not taking any more of this stuff! Interview's over! Get somebody else to answer your questions!'' Finally, just as he's about to get up and leave, he leans back in his chair, gives me a big grin, and starts laughing. The whole thing was an act. He was joking. Instead of saying, ''Well, it's up to my manager, I'll fight anybody he wants,'' Cooney defused the question by acting like he was upset.

Although Cooney doesn't have reservations about hurting people the way Patterson did, he did get a little scared during the fight with Norton in the spring of 1981. Cooney demolished Norton in fifty-four seconds of the first round. It was a dangerous fight because Norton got trapped in a corner against the ropes where Cooney could tee off on him. Norton was out but he couldn't go down all the way because the lower rope was holding him up. If they had let the fight continue, Norton could have been seriously hurt. This frightened

Cooney. "I could see he was finished," Cooney said, "and if I had to continue, I was afraid there'd be permanent damage. I was relieved when the referee came over and said enough."

The thing to remember about this fight, though, is that Cooney didn't back off even when he was scared. You've got to have the killer instinct if you're going to be a great fighter. Some other guy might have looked to the ref a few times and given Norton a break but Cooney kept pounding. He might have been worried about hurting Norton: the killer instinct remained until the referee stopped the fight.

Another guy who made me and the station look good was heavyweight champion Larry Holmes. What a nice guy and an underrated fighter. Certainly it is not his fault there are no bonafide contenders around anymore. He's paid his dues and has been a good champion, ducking no one. Well, one day he's on the 5 p.m. news with me after the Cooney fight and before I can say a thing he says, "Warner Wolf, thank you for picking me to beat Cooney in fifteen rounds [he won in thirteen rounds]. All my friends and I watch you on Channel Two down in Easton, Pennsylvania. Gimme a break and let's go to the videotape." What a great plug from the heavyweight champion of the world!

Now some people say boxing should be abolished. I don't agree. More people have been killed in auto racing than boxing, yet no one says to abolish auto racing. In fact, in auto racing, spectators and crew members have been killed. Sure, the intent in boxing is to hurt your opponent—but it's not to kill your opponent. The intent is to win, any way you can, whether it be knock out your opponent or win on points. Former featherweight champion Willie Pep once won a round in a fight and never threw a punch. That's right, he told a sports writer beforehand that that's what he was going to do and he did it. That's how good Pep was. I think the bottom line is this: Nobody forces people to be boxers or race drivers. It's a free choice by the individual, who selects that profession to make his living by. This is the United States; who are we to deny a person his choice?

Fear in sports is a subject athletes generally don't like to discuss.

It's always there, though. Everybody deals with it in his own private way.

A few years ago I had Lou Brock on the air to talk about base stealing. You wouldn't think there's fear in stealing, but it's present even for a guy like Brock, the greatest base stealer in history in total steals—938 steals lifetime. He had everything down to a science, everything timed in his head. He said it took him something like 3.0 seconds to run from first to second, an average of 1.2 seconds for the pitcher to throw the ball to the catcher, and 2.1 seconds for the catcher to throw to second. That meant he could usually depend on arriving 0.3 seconds ahead of the tag.

But the interesting thing is, of his 938 steals, he stole home only twice. Brock didn't use the word "scared," but the fear of getting hurt was apparently in his mind.

"I tried stealing home in 1962, my rookie year with the Cubs," he said. "We had the sign on, but the batter didn't pick it up. I'm racing down the line ready to steal home when all of a sudden the batter swings and hits a line drive down the third base line. All I could think of, what if the ball hit me flush in the head?" Except for once in 1964 with the Cubs and again in 1970 with the Cardinals against the Mets, Brock never attempted to steal home again.

Obviously, the fear of personal injury has to be number one in sports. These guys' bodies are their security. I remember talking with Bennie Friedman, the old pro quarterback from the Giants and the University of Michigan, who said he knew how not to get hurt.

Friedman was a star with the Giants in the 1930s. I interviewed him a couple years ago when two or three quarterbacks seemed to be getting racked up every week. He said the reason was not that the defensive players were bigger and faster and thus able to hit that much harder, but that the quarterbacks didn't know how to fall.

"Nobody's taught 'em," he said. "In the old days, there was a real art of falling. You'd see 'em coming at you, so you'd curl your body into a ball, sort of like being in the fetal position, and fall. Step two was to consciously relax your bones and muscles, so when they piled on you wouldn't feel it as much. We were skinny guys back then, and we didn't have the fancy equipment of today.

It's just that our coaches taught us from the first day of practice how to fall.''

My own theory is that the football field has become too small for today's players. Quarterbacks in Benny Friedman's day were 5 feet 7 and 150 pounds. Today they're 6 feet 2 and over 200, and the guys hitting them are 6 feet 6 and 280. Plus the defensive guy runs 40 yards in 4.5 to 5 seconds. So you've got a bigger guy, a taller guy, and a faster guy, but the field is the same size. Of course there are more injuries. The players have outgrown the dimensions of the field. One of the first things I would do if I were commissioner of football would be to widen the field and perhaps lengthen it. It's not big enough any more.

I'm sometimes asked how you deal with ball players who would rather not talk—a rapidly multiplying breed these days. My answer is you don't push. I learned this in my first interview with a non-talking player. It was with Richie Allen then with the Phillies in 1976.

''Hi, Dick [he insisted on your calling him Dick], I'm Warner Wolf, ABC Sports. Dick, the first question: After playing in both leagues, what's the difference in the pitching between the two leagues?''

''I'd rather not talk today,'' he said politely.

Sometimes you get a look that tells you follow-up questions are out of order. I quickly formed my Richie Allen Rule: *If player does not want to be interviewed, vacate premises immediately*. Forget him. Saves him time and saves you time. Move on. There are other players who will talk. In fact, some of them will talk so much you can only get a word in during the commercial break. This is when being a sportscaster turns into an absolute joy.

Not being able to squeeze in a word happened to me at Channel 2 when the three great New York center fielders from the 1950s—Mickey Mantle, Willie Mays, and Duke Snider—came on. Only time they've ever been *together* on a television show. The show was moving along so well that halfway through the show, during a commercial, Mantle leans over and says to me, ''They actually *pay* you for this?'' Mantle basically is a shy person who has a great sense of humor.

•

As a fan, I always wanted to know what went through players' minds during long, lopsided games.

"Mickey, all those great teams you played on, I would see the Yankees clobber the Washington Senators, twelve–one, thirteen–two, both ends of a double-header. In all honesty, was it hard concentrating on the game when you were in the field?"

"First time I've ever been asked that," Mantle said. "Sure, it was difficult. Very difficult. You're supposed to keep thinking how much speed the guy on first has and which base you're gonna throw to if you get the ball. No way you can concentrate completely when it's twelve–one. You start thinking about the talk you have to give that night at some banquet. Or maybe your mind is on your wife and kids back in Dallas. The only place where outside stuff has no effect is in the batter's box. The score could be a hundred to one and it wouldn't matter. I would still be able to concentrate enough to hit."

On the *Warner Wolf Show,* when Mantle got together with Mays and Snider, they talked about today's salaries. Unbelievable what they'd make today. If Mantle were playing with the Yankees in New York, he probably would clear $2.5 million a year. The most he made was $100,000. In 1956 Mantle wins the Triple Crown—.353, 52 home runs, 130 runs batted in. In 1957 Mantle hits .365 with 34 home runs, gets 94 RBIs, and leads the league in runs scored with 121. Great year, right? Wrong! Yankee general manager George Weiss wants to cut him $10,000. Weiss says, "Come on Mickey, you gotta take a cut! You hit .365 but you didn't win the Triple Crown again."

It's amazing how stingy the owners were back then. In 1954 Snider finished third in the batting race with an average of .341. The guy had a Hall of Fame year—120 RBIs, 40 homers, caught every fly ball in sight. He goes in to Buzzie Bavasi of the Dodgers that winter and asks for a $15,000 raise, from $40,000 to $55,000. "Come on," Bavasi says. "Look at your stolen bases. In 1953 you stole sixteen. Last season you dropped to six. We'll give you a $7,000 raise and call it a deal." And in those days the player had no choice. Take it, or sit out.

All three guys said Don Drysdale was the meanest pitcher they ever saw. Drysdale might sound charming on TV, but if he didn't like your looks, he might aim one of his 95-mile-per-hour fastballs at your shoulder blades.

Mantle picked Drysdale as the meanest even though he only batted against him in All-Star Games, the 1963 World Series, and spring training. Mays said he never could hit Drysdale because he spent half the time against him lying on his back.

Now it was Snider's turn. He was a teammate of Drysdale's for a number of years. One time the Reds were playing the Dodgers in the LA Coliseum. Snider is in center and Drysdale is on the mound. Frank Robinson is at bat. Walter Alston, the Dodger manager, is motioning for an intentional walk, "Put him on! Put him on!" Drysdale acknowledges the sign, winds up, and hits Robinson with the very first pitch. Later, a number of the Dodgers ask Drysdale what happened. "I figured, why waste four pitches?" Drysdale said. "Hit him with one. Get it over with."

"Duke," I said, "talking about guys getting hit, how about all this violence going on today? You got players going into the stands, fans throwing stuff . . ."

"Not to excuse it, but you'd get some of it back in the fifties, too," he said. "When we used to play at Crosley Field in Cincinnati, they had this crazy habit of allowing the fans out on the field when the game was over. They'd mingle with you as soon as the last out was made. You couldn't run into the dugout because you'd trip over somebody.

"Anyway, we once went into Cincinnati on a five-game losing streak. The local papers said we had been choking on the tight ones. If the Reds made it close, they would find us 'gutless,' the headlines said.

"As it turns out, we win the game, six–five, in twelve innings. I catch the ball for the final out, I start running in, and here come the fans. This guy runs up to me and says, 'Snider, you know something? You're gutless.' Same word as in the newspapers. The guy isn't even original. Suddenly, he hauls off and takes a punch at me. I duck under it and with my glove hand—I still had my glove on—I decked him with a left hook to the mouth. Boom! Down he goes onto the grass.

"I didn't think much more of it until I got a summons that night at the hotel. 'Edwin D. Snider, you are hereby ordered to appear at Court of General Sessions, First District, City of Cincinnati, 10 a.m.' I couldn't believe this was happening. Here this guy who tried to attack me is accusing me of assaulting him. I round up Carl Furillo, our right fielder, as a witness, and the next morning we go down to the courthouse.

"It turns out the guy was six feet six—I figured what on earth did I hit *him* for—and had been in jail all night. The cops must have taken him away the moment I decked him. Birdie Tebbetts, the Reds' manager, was there as a second witness.

"The judge says, 'All right, fellas, what's the story here?' We both explain what happened. The judge deliberates for about three seconds and says to the fan, 'Well, sir, you took the first swing. And Mr. Snider, you took the second. I call it a draw. I'm willing to forget the whole thing.'

" 'Oh, yeah?' the fan yells. 'Just wait a minute! What about my bridgework here? What about the crack he put in my tooth?' The guy puts his finger in his mouth and starts tapping on one of his teeth.

" 'I'm no dentist! I'm a judge!' is the reply.

"Boom! 'Case dismissed.' "

13

Monday Night Baseball

Before I tell you about *Monday Night Baseball,* let me tell you about how I passed the audition. I was asked to come to New York to do a Mets-Phillies game at Shea Stadium. Night game, September 1975, I flew up to New York City that afternoon with my wife. All week I had prepared for the game. I knew every Met and Phillies player backwards and forwards. I had saved the entire year's issues of *The Sporting News.* I was prepared. I knew what every player did in all the Phillies-Mets games played that year. Herb Granath, a VP of ABC-TV Sports, took me under his wing during the audition. He sat me in a corner of the mezzanine, gave me a mike, I did the game, and he taped my play-by-play. After the game, Herb took my wife and me to P. J. Clarke's restaurant. I remember, traffic was so bad that night that Herb's chauffeur, Murray, actually drove on the sidewalk one block to avoid a traffic jam. All I could think of was "only in New York." Apparently ABC liked the audition. In March 1976, they told me I was one of their three announcers on the "A" team of *Monday Night Baseball.* Bob Prince, Bob Uecker, and me.

However, within three months I knew deep down it just wasn't going to work. The date was June 28, 1976. I'm in Detroit to do the Monday Night game between the Tigers and the Yankees. Bob Uecker, my broadcast partner, comes to me that morning. "Warner," he says, "you're not gonna believe this. The Tigers are gonna start a kid who has conversations with the ball between pitches. The guy's unreal. He kneels down and smooths out the dirt on the mound. He runs out and shakes hands with the shortstop. I guarantee you've never seen anything like him. Mark Fidrych, pronounced FID-rich. They call him 'The Bird' after the *Sesame Street* character."

Later that morning we have a meeting to determine the opening of the show. The chief producer of *Monday Night Baseball* starts giving orders. "Kenny Holtzman is pitching for the Yankees," he says. "Gotta open the show with Holtzman."

"Uh, listen, I think we might be missin' a story here," I said.

"What's that?"

I repeat what Uecker told me. "Look," I said, "I've never seen this Bird guy either, but he's gotta be sensational. The park is sold out already. People are lined up to buy standing room. It's phenomenal. They're not coming to see Holtzman, they're all coming because of this kid."

The name Fidrych meant nothing to the producer. "Warner," he says, "you don't understand. We only open with the big names here. Guys like O. J. Simpson in football, Pete Rose or Johnny Bench in baseball. Nobody knows who Mark Fidrych is."

"Of course they don't know now. But they will after tonight. When we go on, show Fidrych warming up. I'll come on, and say, 'This is twenty-year-old Mark Fidrych. He has a record of six and one. Talks to the ball, rubs the mound, congratulates the shortstop, leads the league in earned-run average. Fifty thousand people have come to Tiger Stadium to see him pitch!' BOOM! That's it. If that opening doesn't hold an audience, nothing's gonna hold 'em."

The producer says, "No good. Need a name. We're going with Holtzman."

That afternoon I call up my wife. "Hon," I say, "I don't think I'm going to get along here. The producer's wrong, and the worst part is, he's missing a story."

Finally the broadcast begins. Uecker does play-by-play for the first three innings, Bob Prince does the middle three, and I do the seventh, eighth, and ninth. Top of the ninth, and the Bird is beating the Yankees 5–1. He gets the first two batters, Graig Nettles and Oscar Gamble. The crowd is now on its feet. Fidrych is rubbing up the ball and talking to it at the same time. You can see his lips moving. Incredible! "Ladies and gentlemen," I say, "if Fidrych gets the final out, the crowd is going to go crazy!"

The Bird kneels down and smooths out the mound. He rubs up the ball, telling it to go over the outside of the plate and dip low just as it reaches the batter. You can see Fidrych talking to the ball. The pitch to Elrod Hendricks: ground ball to short, throw to first, game's over. BOOM! Tiger Stadium fans go crazy. The Bird is jumping up and down shaking hands with each player as he comes off the field and into the dugout. The fans are cheering as if it was the seventh game of the World Series. "Folks," I say, "they're not going to stop clapping until The Bird comes back from the dugout." Lately, curtain calls have become common. But back then in 1976, this may have been the first one on national TV. Finally, Fidrych sticks his head back out, curls and all, and waves. The crowd goes even wilder. "This is fantastic!" I say. "Mark Fidrych is born tonight on coast-to-coast television!" It had to be one of the truly great moments of sports on television. Overnight The Bird became a national sensation.

All right, good broadcast. Good feeling. Everybody says thank you very much. The next week, I arrange a meeting with the producer.

"Now that the game is over," I say, "and having the benefit of hindsight about Fidrych, would you have opened with him?"

"Oh, no, no," the producer goes. "Remember what I said last week? Big names? We open with big names here. O. J. Simpson, Pete Rose, Johnny Bench."

"In other words, no mistake? You don't think you might have missed a story here?"

"Oh, no, no. Of course not. Fidrych wasn't a name then."

From that point on, my career in network television went more or less downhill, although I think they were happy with my work at the winter and summer Olympics that year. However, I never knew for sure because they usually didn't tell you how you were doing one way or the other. I will say I was excited, and that's usually an indication to me that I'm coming across. They had me do the speed skating from Innsbruck and the bicycle racing from Montreal. Good assignments, because they were fast-moving, exciting events.

But I probably should have realized the baseball play-by-play wouldn't work. Not only was it difficult working for a network that tried to change your style, but blaming no one but myself, I couldn't always keep up my interest while announcing baseball if it wasn't a good ball game.

The first time I noticed this was when I was working for WTOP-TV in Washington—a Senators-Twins game from Minnesota in 1970. It was a battle for last place, played before a handful of fans on a Sunday afternoon. Not a cloud in the sky. Seventy degrees. All I could think of was, I'd rather be back in Washington playing softball with my friends.

I got the same feeling at ABC a few months after the Fidrych game. Uecker, Prince, and I were doing an Orioles-Twins game out of Minnesota. August 1976. The Twins were about ten games out of first place and the Orioles were eleven out. The score was 8–1, Baltimore. The last three innings, I'm doing the play-by-play. ''Except for Baltimore fans, who cares about this game?'' I'm thinking. ''Who's watching? I wouldn't be watching this if I were home.'' I began thinking, man, if it was this difficult for me to get excited about a one-sided game, I wasn't going to be a very successful play-by-play man.

Now, doing a boring game is bad enough, but when you're cold and you desperately need to leave the booth, it's even worse. Two of the coldest situations I've ever been in in my life were, one, when I did the world speed-skating championships in a place called Heerenveen, Holland, and two, a Giants game in San Francisco. In Holland, I had a wool coat, two blankets, and long johns, and I was in a booth which was not heated. For three hours I did the speed skating with the blankets wrapped around me. It felt like 0°; I was frozen.

Then in June 1977 I did a *Monday Night Baseball* game from

San Francisco. Cubs versus the Giants in windy Candlestick Park. I had now been bumped down to the "B" team. I couldn't go to the bathroom because I had to do all the play-by-play. Terrible experience! Cold and I had to go to the bathroom. Plus it turned out to be a fourteen-inning game. It was like, "Let me outta here! Let me go!" The only thing you can do is hold it in. Don't drink anything, that's for sure. Terrible! Couldn't concentrate on the game. Couldn't wait for it to be over. There were only 4,000 people in the stands watching two bad ball clubs.

The first year on *Monday Night Baseball* should have been fun but wasn't. Let me say this: Uecker, Prince, and I were not the greatest on-air combination. But we always got along well, especially the one week the number one producer happened to be gone. We were all saying to ourselves, "Hey, this is the way it should be." The producer got back the next week and we told him how great it had been. "I know why it was a lot of fun," he said. "Because the other producer let you do what you wanted."

Now one problem you'd have doing a ball game is that while you'd be talking on the air, the producer in the truck would be talking in your ear. Since you were on the air and couldn't talk back to him, except between innings, it was a one-way conversation with him doing all the talking. He wanted your attention *at that moment*. Maybe he'd shout so you could hear him better. "Hey!" he'd yell, "I thought I told you to talk about what we've got on *Wide World* this week."

Let's suppose Uecker or Prince is asking me a question on the air. I'm trying to hear what Uecker or Prince is saying so I can respond, but meanwhile the producer is shouting in our ears. I remember once I had to ask Uecker on the air to repeat his question because the producer had been talking in my ear at the same time.

Looking back, some of the things that happened on *Monday Night Baseball* that first year were almost comical. People would never believe the back-and-forth communication between the booth and the truck.

One part of your job as a play-by-play man is reading promos. We were doing a Pirates-Reds game from Cincinnati my first year.

ABC was to carry the PGA golf championship a few days later, and I had the duty of hyping it. They'd give you cue cards: ''Next week, live and exclusive! The PGA golf tournament from Duluth, Georgia. Friday, Saturday, Sunday! Right here on ABC Sports!'' I read it *before* my first inning of play-by-play and *after* my first inning. After my second inning, the producer says, ''Read it again.'' That made three times in two innings.

After my third inning, he's back on my earphones.

''I want you to read that again,'' he says.

''I won't read it again,'' I tell him. ''Let Prince read it or Uecker read it.''

''I asked *you*. Why won't *you* read it?''

''Because I can't. I've plugged it enough. I've promoted the thing for the last time. I'm beginning to feel like a shill.''

All right, fine. Next inning, Prince reads it. He sounds good. Great reading job. Terrific. I'm glad Prince is reading it. Except at the end he gets this gleam in his eye, turns to me and says, ''Warner, what do you think of the PGA?''

''Truthfully, Bob, I don't play golf. And I've never belonged to a country club.''

After the game I was going back to the hotel when I saw the producer. ''You know, you really hurt yourself with that one,'' he said.

''Hey, that's how I felt,'' I said.

I'll tell you another disagreement I had with the producer. July 5, 1976, the week after the Fidrych game. We're in Philadelphia for the Phillies against the Dodgers. The Phillies have just returned home in first place after a ten-game road trip. They're meeting the Dodgers, one of the best teams in the West. That morning we go to the producer's room for the production meeting. Everybody's batting around ideas for the opening.

''I think we ought to give 'em something like this,'' I said. ''Camera pans around the stadium, theme music begins. I go, 'Ladies and gentlemen, you're looking at sixty thousand fans in Veterans' Stadium, Philadelphia. The fans in this park are here to welcome home the hottest team in baseball.' ''

"You mean you want to emphasize the winning streak?" the producer says. "Don't be silly. That's not why the fans are here. They're here because yesterday was the Bicentennial. They want to see the fireworks display."

It just so happens that ABC was going to televise the fireworks display at the end of the game, and part of his job was to keep reminding the viewers of that. So go big with the fireworks and the Fourth of July angle, he said.

I compromised and mentioned both the winning streak and the fireworks. It made everyone happy.

Several weeks later we're in Kansas City for the Angels against the Royals. It's late August 1976, normally the time of year the pennant races heat up. Only this year it was all over. Yankees, Royals, Reds, Phillies. They had the races locked up weeks in advance. We get together for the production meeting. The producer starts issuing orders.

"I want you guys to point out all the great comebacks like the 1951 Giants who were thirteen games out, the 1942 Cardinals, ten and a half out, that sort of stuff," he says. "Gotta drum up some excitement out there. These viewers are losing interest in the races."

Prince, Uecker, and I couldn't believe it. We all refused. "Look," I said, "the races are over. O–V–E–R, over. The fans aren't dumb. Who's gonna catch the Royals? The White Sox? The Rangers?" By this time I was also doing the 6 o'clock sports at WABC-TV in New York. I'd already given my opinion that the races were over. All of a sudden I'm supposed to change now on national television? I'm supposed to say, "Wait a minute! Watch out! Remember the 1951 Giants?" Come on, forget it. We all refused.

Two days later *Sports Illustrated* comes out with a story on great baseball comebacks. The producer may have gotten word from someone at the magazine. All about the 1951 Giants and the 1942 Cardinals. I think he was upset not being ahead of the story. Next week's meeting, he's got the magazine in hand. "You guys see this?" he says. "This is exactly what I was trying to tell you!"

"So what if *Sports Illustrated* had the story?" I say. "That's supposed to make it right? Just because *Sports Illustrated* says something, we have to act like a parrot on *Monday Night Baseball*?''

We fought like this the whole year. It was bad. I knew this wasn't the way it was supposed to be. Broadcasting was supposed to be fun, and this wasn't.

Cincinnati, summer of the 1976 season. Cubs against the Reds. Once again it's my job to set the theme in the opening. I figure, well, the Reds have beaten the Cubs seventeen of the last eighteen times. Gary Nolan, who won fifteen for the Reds that year, going for the eventual World Series champions.

As I'm about to go on the air, the president of ABC Sports gets on the earphone and says, ''Don't mention the Reds' domination over the Cubs.''

''But it's true!'' I tell him.

''Yeah, but it might turn away some of our viewers,'' he says.

''The audience isn't dumb. The baseball fan knows. The Cubs are in last place and the Reds are in first place. The Cubs are nineteen games behind.''

''Hey,'' he says, ''the Cubs are playing good ball now.''

''You mean the two out of three they won in San Francisco?''

''Well,'' he says, ''that's what you want to play up.''

So, I went on the air and said, ''Cincinnati Reds versus Chicago Cubs! Cubs lost seventeen out of eighteen to the Reds over the last two years, but the Cubs are coming in here after winning two out of three in San Francisco over the weekend.'' Moral of the story: same as the Phillies-Dodgers fireworks illustration. Sometimes there can be a compromise, as long as you don't compromise *yourself*. You can't fool the audience. The Reds won the game, by the way, 3–2.

The following year I'm doing a Braves-Phillies backup game that was televised to only a few regions of the country. The Braves are owned by Ted Turner, the cable-TV guy who is big on yachting. That morning the producer—a different one than the first-string producer I was used to working with—says that during the game he's going to run a film of Turner on his boat. ''I want you to do the voice-over,'' he says, meaning I would read a narration over the film.

"I'd rather not narrate yachting," I said. "I don't know anything about it, and I don't want to fake it. Get somebody else. Ask my broadcast partner if he would like to read it."

"I'm the producer," the guy says. "Are *you* telling *me* what to play?"

"Oh, no—look, play it," I say. "You're right. You *are* the producer. It's your game. But as an announcer, I'm not voicing-over this piece. I want nothing to do with it."

"If you don't voice it over," he says, "how can I play it?"

"That's for you to decide. You either play it by itself or ask someone else to read the voice-over."

Half an hour before the game I'm walking up to the booth when I run into the producer. "This is your last chance to read the voice-over," he says.

"No," I tell him, "my answer is no."

The following is a verbatim quote: "You leave me no alternative," he says. "I will have to report this to higher authorities."

I put my hands up like it was a holdup. "Am I under arrest?" I ask.

I don't think he thought that was funny. I did only one more *Monday Night Baseball* game before I became a nonperson. I suppose the producer and the president of ABC Sports thought I was a rebel.

Now I'm going to tell you about one of the most unpleasant assignments I've ever had in broadcasting, an assignment which I briefly touched upon earlier.

October 14, 1976. Final game of the American League playoffs, Yankees against the Royals, Yankee Stadium. Whoever wins goes to the World Series. Yankees are ahead, 6–3, top of the eighth. Up steps George Brett. BOOM! Three-run homer, upper deck, ties the score. Next inning the president orders Uecker and me to go down under the stands to the ABC press room next door to the dressing rooms. The minute the game is over, Uecker and I are supposed to pounce on the players for interviews. Uecker is to take the winners, I'm to take the losers.

I get to the press room, sit down in the chair, and start looking at the TV monitor. Bottom of the ninth. Mark Littell pitches to

Chris Chambliss. BOOM! There it goes! Over the wall, home run! Yankees win the pennant! You can see Chambliss trampling over fans as he tries to run around the bases. Everybody's screaming in the press room. You can feel the stands vibrate from the fans banging on the concrete steps above. Incredible scene to a Yankee fan; one of the most dramatic home runs in the history of baseball.

"Get over to the Royals," the president says. "Try to get Littell on. Try to get Brett."

I want you to picture how it is in the Kansas City dressing room. The players are still coming in. It's like a funeral. Nobody's talking. Heads bowed and some guys are crying. Here I come in with the television cameras. My crew has to set up. "Excuse me," they say to one of the players. "Mind if we put our lighting fixtures here?" The place was exactly like a morgue. Not that the Royals had never lost a dramatic game, but it was the *way* they lost this one. It wasn't like the bases had been loaded and everybody was ready. The game had been tied. First pitch, last of the ninth—BOOM!—pennant's over. These guys were still in shock.

I never looked at anybody in there. Just heard the voices.

"C'mon, get outta here!"

"Whaddya think this place is, a theater?"

I was sort of glad I couldn't find Littell. He was probably in the trainer's room, which is off limits to the media. But I saw Brett on his stool in the corner, so I went over to him. He was looking at his feet. The crew starts adjusting the lights.

"George," I said, "too bad, you guys played well . . ."

Brett just looked down at the floor and nodded. Didn't say a thing. I mean, why should he say a thing? He just wanted to be left alone. This was a deeply personal moment for him. You could see there were tears in his eyes.

"George," I went on, "up until Chambliss hit his homer, you were the hero. You brought 'em back . . ."

"That's right," he said vacantly, raising his head and staring at me.

"George, tell us about that homer of yours in the eighth. Were you trying to hit it out? Were you goin' for it?"

There was a long pause. Maybe five seconds, which can be an

eternity in television. Finally Brett took a deep sigh. ''Yeah,'' he said, ''sure was. Two on, down by three—I was trying to hit it out.''

''Gee,'' I said, ''I know this must be a tough moment for you to go through . . .''

Brett didn't say another word. Too often we perhaps forget that athletes are also human beings with human feelings.

I believe there's no way you should walk through a clubhouse door before the players have gathered control of themselves and had a moment of privacy.

It took me a long time to get over that interview. The more I thought about it, the more it bothered me. At home the next day, I sat down and wrote a letter to Brett.

''Dear George,'' I said, ''I want to apologize for the imposition and thank you for answering my questions. I know it was really a rough time for you and your teammates. Your friend, Warner Wolf.''

The next season I saw Brett at one of the games. He said he appreciated the letter and that he understood the circumstances.

''Warner, the biggest thing about the note was that it was written in your own hand,'' he said. ''You didn't have a secretary do it.''

''George,'' I replied, ''I don't have a secretary.'' We both laughed, but it's the truth, even today. No secretary. No typewriter. My philosophy is write it out longhand, do it yourself.

14

In the Network Doghouse

I've always said you can't be a success until you've been a failure. Not only in television, but in life. Man, unless you've failed, you don't have anything to compare the success to. There's no way you can understand or appreciate it.

Let's say you went into the business, radio/television, and you caught on right away. You went right to the network, never worked in a small-town station, never had to read the news at 6 a.m. on Sunday. You had some appeal that everybody liked, so you went right to the top. How could you truly enjoy the value of that? How could you measure it? Sure, you'd get some financial reward or adulation from the people, but there would be no foundation underneath it.

A television performer who has never gone through the experience of being fired, never was replaced on the air, or never went through bad ratings just doesn't *know*. Those are cruel blows at the time. You remember them. But if you've worked your way up and failed somewhere along the way, then you're in position to be thankful when you are successful. You not only know the difference, you can appreciate the difference.

So failure is all right. It has its purpose. Nothing wrong with failure if you can pick yourself up and succeed after that.

I didn't realize it at the time, but it was during my down period at the network that I began thinking like this. I had so much time on my hands after *Monday Night Baseball* in 1976 that I could have taken up shuffleboard. In 1977 they put me first on the ''B'' team and then on the ''C'' team in baseball. I did three games all summer. There was no more *College Football Scoreboard* after 1976. Fewer and fewer *Wide World of Sports* assignments. They don't talk to you or even acknowledge that you are on the payroll. The only way you know is when you get your paycheck.

You have to understand that this was little more than a year after I went to ABC, the very time my career was supposed to be taking off. Beginning in 1977, I started getting fewer and fewer assignments. I still had the 6 o'clock sports at WABC. But between June 1977 and March 1978, the month the network part of my contract expired, I had only two assignments—a Phillies-Braves game in August '77 and a Dodgers-Padres game that Labor Day.

I learned a lesson during this period: If you're not happy in your work, then you're not going to be happy at home. Man, you've got to have a good wife during a time like this. Because all I ever did was complain. I was drifting career-wise and I knew it. I'd complain around the clock: ''What's going on here? They're not using me. Why do they try to change me? Didn't they know what they were getting? Why aren't they putting me on the air?''

On and on it went. If your career isn't going well, the worst thing that can happen is for you to have time on your hands, because then you dwell on it. I began thinking I should just quit and try to go back to Washington . . . if any station would have me. But, hey, maybe it was too late. And if they did take me back, would the public be the same? Who's to say they wouldn't resent me for leaving? The alternative, though, seemed even worse. What was I to do, keep marking time in New York?

Finally I said to Sue, ''Hey, this is ridiculous. Why don't I just quit and see what happens. Maybe they'll take me back in Washington and maybe not. But staying here is absurd. I'm getting paid for doing nothing, and something for nothing is nothing.''

''Look,'' she said, ''play out the string. The contract is up in March. Finish the contract, let it expire, and then if you want to go back to Washington or someplace else, nobody will be able to call you a quitter.''

If it wasn't for my wife I wouldn't be in New York right now.

The thing that troubled me the most and left the worst taste in my mouth was receiving money for doing virtually nothing. They were paying me a big salary, but I had only three assignments—the Ping-Pong tournament and those two baseball games—from April of 1977 to March of 1978. I mean, it wasn't that I was stealing, because I still had a valid contract with them. But they were paying me, in effect, to sit. ''Going on the beach,'' we call it in the TV business. Like paying a football coach not to coach after being fired. I couldn't get it out of my head what a waste of money this was. Three assignments: in effect they paid me $50,000 per assignment. Think of it. This is absolutely crazy. What kind of a way to run a business is this?

Let this be a reminder if you ever work for a network: Just because you're getting paid doesn't mean they'll use you. The lesson here is: When you do sign a contract, make sure the assignments are included in the contract.

People think the networks always proceed very carefully, that they review a guy's work very thoroughly, scout him, and then hire him because they know exactly why he succeeds. ''Hey, look at this guy, he's hot in Washington, let's grab him,'' they say, but sometimes they do so without stopping to think *why* he's hot.

Besides *Monday Night Baseball*, one of the first things to go wrong for me was the *College Football Scoreboard* show, the studio show after the Saturday afternoon football game was over in which I would give the scores and offer a comment. It seemed, however, ABC just wanted the scores. Appalachian State 28, Bowling Green 21. Never mind any commentary or ad-lib remarks. Just read the scores. That way neither the sponsors nor the National Collegiate Athletic Association, which sold the rights to the football games at ABC, would get upset.

My first year on the scoreboard was the fall of 1975. I had just signed the contract with ABC and was still working at Channel 9 in Washington, flying up to New York on weekends. Late in

September, Ohio State is playing UCLA. Ohio State is winning, 38–20, less than one minute left in the game. Woody Hayes orders a field goal! The kick is good, and Ohio State wins 41–20 instead of 38–20.

I come on with the scoreboard show right after the game. ''The Boo of the Week,'' I say, ''goes to Mr. Woody Hayes for kicking a field goal that late in the game with an eighteen-point lead. Two things you don't do under the circumstances: You don't pass and you don't kick a field goal. You run the ball. If you run and they can't hold you, well, you're not to blame. But you don't kick a field goal with an eighteen-point lead, and less than one minute to play. Boo on Woody Hayes!''

I start hearing from the Ohio State Alumni Association, all the Buckeye boosters in the midwest, all the military history buffs who think Woody Hayes is one part Patton, one part Julius Caesar, and one part greatest football coach of all time. Unbelievable, the amount of reaction. You'd think I had taken a shot at motherhood!

One month later, Alabama, which was undefeated, was playing Texas Christian University, which had lost fifteen in a row. Alabama is winning, 35–0, with three minutes to go in the third quarter when Bear Bryant, just like Woody Hayes, orders a field goal. Here we go again! BOOM. The field goal was good, the score becomes 38–0 Alabama and Alabama goes on to win, 45–0.

I come on with the same criticism I used for Hayes. ''Boo of the Week goes to Bear Bryant for piling it on! Totally ridiculous. Five-touchdown lead, little more than a quarter to go, and against a team that has lost fifteen in a row. It appears some coaches pile up the score just to influence the guys who vote in the football polls.''

Holy Moses, what a reaction! Two days later I get a letter from the Alabama Alumni Association. The guy starts defending the Bear.

''If we had run the ball,'' he says, ''we would have scored a touchdown and the score would've been even higher. So we had to kick the field goal. We were doing TCU a favor by limiting ourselves to three points.'' How's that for incredible reasoning?

A few months later, the committee that awards the Heisman

Trophy to the best college football player in the nation gives it to Ohio State's Archie Griffin. He had also won the trophy in 1974.

I go on the air and say, "Boo of the Week to the committee that picked Archie Griffin! Hey, nothing wrong with Griffin. Great player, four-year statistics are outstanding. But five guys outgained Griffin in total yardage this year—Ricky Bell of USC, Herb Lusk of Long Beach State, Tony Dorsett of Pitt, Chuck Muncie of California, and Louie Giammona of Utah State. *And,* they didn't play on as great a team as Ohio State. I'm afraid the people who voted were influenced by Griffin's four-year statistics rather than by what he's done this year alone, which is supposed to be the rule."

If the letter writers were furious before, now they really went out of their minds. A lot of people thought I was picking on Ohio State because I had given out two Boos that had to do with their coach and star player. Hey, gimme a break! It just happened to turn out that way. It could have been any school.

The next season, 1976, I continued to give my opinions and an occasional Boo of the Week. However, in February 1977 two vice presidents from ABC Sports, John Lazarus and Herb Granath, came in for a visit. Now Granath, whom I had known since my *Monday Night Baseball* audition a year and a half before, did take an honest interest in my career and seemed to care how I was doing. I was getting ready to do a sportscast for the local station, Channel 7, when they walked in, sat down, and asked if it was possible not to do any more Boos of the Week on the *Scoreboard* show. Then and there I knew I didn't have too many days left on that show. Little did I realize I had none. That August they officially told me I had done my last *Scoreboard* show.

I'll never forget the last week of April 1976. I'm still under contract to the ABC network, plus I'm doing my side appearances on the 6 o'clock news for WABC. Remember, Channel 7 in New York is wholly owned and operated by the ABC network. I go on the sports and say, "This weekend on ABC you're going to see Honest Pleasure in the Kentucky Derby and Jimmy Young versus Muhammad Ali for the heavyweight championship of the world.

All I can say is Jimmy Young has about as much chance of beating Muhammad Ali as the other ten horses have of beating Honest Pleasure. In other words, *none*.'' Then I laughed, signed off, left the station, and went home.

I got home about 7:30, day's work done. I'm sitting down to a nice dinner with my wife and family. Suddenly the phone rings. My wife answers it. ''It's for you,'' she says. I grab the phone and it's the president of ABC Sports.

''Warner,'' he says, ''in one sentence you shot down two of the greatest events we have coming up this week. What are you doing? You work for us, you're on our team. You can't go around knocking off two of our events with one shot. Knock the other networks.''

''Look,'' I tell him, ''I didn't mean anything by it and I wasn't out to shoot down your two events. But it's the truth. You know and I know Ali is gonna beat Young and Honest Pleasure is gonna win the Derby.''

After the conversation I really started thinking. ''Hey, what is this nonsense?'' I thought. ''You knew I was outspoken when you hired me. You knew what you were getting. If you didn't like it, you shouldn't have hired me. But once you hired me, don't call me and try to change my style.''

That Friday night, Ali beats Jimmy Young, although it was a controversial decision and the irony is, the next day Honest Pleasure loses to Bold Forbes by a length.

In February 1976, I'm doing play-by-play of the speed-skating events at the winter Olympics from Innsbruck, Austria. Good assignment. Very exciting and no dead spots. However, one of the first things to go wrong was my smile. After doing a couple of races I say, ''There goes Sheila Young—across the finish line! Great race!'' After summing it up, I go, ''This is Warner Wolf,'' give everybody a smile, and send it back to Jim McKay.

''Get rid of that smile at the end,'' a producer says after I am finished. ''Looks out of place. We don't do that here.''

''Well,'' I said, ''it's kind of a trademark. I'm happy doing the Olympics, I like the assignment. I figure why not let the people know about it . . .''

"I said it looks out of place. This is the Olympics, not the circus," the guy says.

In July, I'm doing a wrap-up show from the summer Olympics in Montreal, from 11:30 to 11:45 p.m. I thought everything went fine the first night we did it. We edited all the footage of the day, recapping the important events. We went right on the air with it. Great highlights. The only problem, I'm told the next day by our producer that the ABC Sports president doesn't want me using so much videotape from that day's events because our fifteen-minute recap might detract from ABC's full coverage from 8 to 11.

From that point on we changed our plan. I would watch the Canadian Broadcasting Corporation's coverage live that afternoon, picking out odds and ends I figured ABC wouldn't use between 8 and 11. If ABC was going to show rowing, I might pick an offbeat boxing match from the CBC feed. The idea was to avoid the highlights viewers saw earlier in the evening from 8 to 11.

One of the clips I showed was a fifteen-second excerpt of a fight between a Russian and a Cuban. Midway through the fight the Russian guy winds up and delivers a vicious right to the Cuban's groin. Low blow! I mean, no way the Russian guy's aim was that bad. I'll never forget the look on the Cuban guy's face. He grabs himself. Ahh, geez, he's in agony, he's throwing back his head, he's hoping the ref will give him a break.

This was one of the few times, network-wise, I was really able to do my own thing. I go on the air and say, "You want to see a foul? Watch this: BOOM!" The Russian guy winds up and hits the Cuban guy in the groin. "The Boo of the Week," I say. Later my producer says it wouldn't be a good idea to take any more shots at the Russians. He speculated that the president of ABC Sports may have been thinking about the possibility of televising the 1980 Olympics to be held in Moscow, and didn't want to do anything to offend the Russians.

In February 1977, a year after the winter Olympics, I went back to Innsbruck. ABC sent me there to do a skiing race for *Wide World*. All right, not bad. In and out, stayed in the hotel, went out to the hill a few times, did the race, and came back to New York to do the voice-over for the skiing piece. We had all this footage of the hill, the town, Pierre Salinger's favorite restaurant—all the places viewers saw the previous year during the Olympics.

"All right, Warner," the producer says, "on the voice-over here, let's tell the people how great it was to return to Innsbruck, which was ABC Sports' home for an entire month in 1976."

I looked at the guy like he was joking. It almost seemed like he was reading an instruction sheet to me off a cue card. I said, "It wasn't very great being in Innsbruck this time compared to the last time. How could it be? It wasn't the Olympics. No way I'm going to say that. My feeling going back there was a two compared to a ten. Nobody was there, no Olympics, no nothing."

"Warner, that's just not the way we do it here," the producer said. "This is *Wide World of Sports*. It's great when we send you back over there, especially if the viewers remember we were there the year before. We're going to open up the show with the mountains and all . . ."

"Listen," I told him, "if you want a travelogue, go call James J. Fitzpatrick, the guy who used to do the short subjects in the movie theaters."

I think the producer might have been too young to remember Fitzpatrick, because he had sort of a blank look when I told him. Apparently he passed on what I said to the higher-ups. Because if they had been getting angry at me gradually, now they were infuriated. *Monday Night Baseball* already had put me in disfavor. Now my reputation for not getting along with producers was cast in concrete.

Another problem I have had over the years is seeing eye to eye with some advertising agencies and promotion departments. In 1978, after I joined WABC full time on the 6 and 11 o'clock news, the station hired an outside ad agency to do some promotional shots of me. For some reason, some promotion departments always try to show you in a different light than you're seen in on the air.

First the ad agency tried to take me out to Central Park. The idea of the promo was going to be, "Oh, here is Warner Wolf playing ball in the park with some kids." The only problem was I hadn't been to the park playing ball with the kids. It just wasn't true, so I said no thanks, please show excerpts from my show if you want to do a promo.

The ad agency comes back and says, ''Warner, how about some shots of you at home with your wife and kids?'' The idea was going to be, ''Here's Warner at home. See how much fun he has in his den.'' I said, ''No thanks, I really don't want your cameras in my home. Besides, the best promo always comes straight from the show.'' Think about this for a minute. You go to a movie theater and what do you see in the coming attractions? Paul Newman playing a role in a movie—the movie you may see in the future. You don't see Paul Newman with his wife at the shore. You don't see Paul Newman eating a pizza. Come on, you see Paul Newman doing what he does best. Parts from the upcoming movie, the previews.

''Nah, nah, this is the advertising business,'' they said. ''We don't do it that way.''

Believe it or not, they came back a third time. This was later in the year after Reggie Jackson and some candy company came out with a chocolate and caramel ''Reggie!'' bar. Two advertising guys walk into my office and say, ''Wow, have we got a great idea for you! We're going to take you on the set and put a camera on you. And when we give the cue, you're going to hold up this unmarked candy bar we have right here and say, 'Someday they're going to name a candy bar after me! They'll call it the 'Warner!' bar or the 'Wolf' bar.''

''No way! No way!'' I yelled. ''I can't believe you guys would come in here and propose that. Absolutely not!''

''Why not?'' they said.

''Because it's an obvious copy of Reggie Jackson. Forget it. Get the candy bar out of your head. That's not me. I'll go on the set and let you shoot me on the show, but none of this candy bar stuff. Besides, mothers everywhere will accuse me of helping their kids get cavities.''

The following day, they come in to shoot the promo. Predictably, just as they're about to shoot, one guy whips a candy bar out of his pocket and tries to stick it in my hand. ''Just in case you changed your mind,'' he says.

Ironically, the very next night Reggie Jackson refuses Billy

Martin's orders to bunt in an extra-inning game at Yankee Stadium. He gets fined, suspended, and receives even worse publicity than he received the year before in Boston when Martin accused him of failing to hustle after a fly ball which went for a base hit. All I could think of was, if I had gone through with the "Warner!" bar ad, the viewers would have associated me with Reggie and his candy bar. The timing would have been awful.

I guess I should be thankful that WABC was at least interested enough in me to do a promo. Because by the summer of 1977, I had gone into a total eclipse of the moon at the network level. My last major event had been the Phillies-Reds National League playoffs in October 1976.

I did everything I could to find out what was going wrong, but no one would give me an answer. I wrote to the president of ABC Sports. I tried to call the president. No response, except for, "He's out of town," or "He's busy," or "He's in a conference right now," *and* the old standby, "He'll call you back." Of course, he never called back.

One morning, in the midst of this situation, I woke up and went into the bathroom to shave. I'll never forget the day. June 1, 1977. I had had practically no assignments since October 1976. I looked in the mirror and picked up my electric razor. "You know," I said to myself, "this is it. I'm just going to go over there and have it out." The ABC building was at 1330 Avenue of the Americas—Sixth Avenue and 54th Street. It took ten minutes by taxi. I didn't know whether he was in his office or even in New York. I just said enough is enough, finished shaving, and hailed a cab.

I take the elevator to the twenty-fourth floor and walk into his outer office.

"Excuse me," I say. "I want to see the president."

The secretary looks at her sheet and says, "You don't have an appointment."

"I know."

"Well, he can't see you if you don't have an appointment."

"I'm not leaving till he sees me," I say.

"What do you mean?"

"I mean I'm not leaving till he sees me."

"But you don't understand. He's in there with important people . . ."

"Fine. He can take all the time he wants. All afternoon, all day tomorrow, I don't care. I'm not leaving till he sees me."

The great thing about his office was that it had only one entrance and one exit: *the same*. He was trapped. I knew it; the secretary knew it. The only way for him not to see me was to jump out the window onto Sixth Avenue. Finally, the secretary goes into his office, comes out, and says, "I'm sorry, but he's just not going to see you today."

"Fine." I sit down and say, "I'm waiting till he sees me."

Now an hour goes by. She goes in again, comes out, and says, "He's still with those important people. He says he'll give you a call."

"No way!" I tell her. "I'm not leaving till I see him. I just want to know where I stand." You see, I had absolutely nothing to lose. I wasn't doing anything for ABC anyway. It wasn't like he could take any assignments away from me. I had none to take away. I just wanted to know where I stood.

The president had this young guy who ran errands for him. About an hour later this guy comes out of the office and says, "The president says he'll call you tonight."

"Forget it," I say. "I'd prefer to see him in person. I'm better in face-to-face interviews."

Another hour goes by. The same guy comes out again. "The president wants to read *The Washingtonian* article about you first," he says. (The guy's referring to a magazine story about me at ABC that ran in *The Washingtonian* a month before, saying, "Whatever happened to Warner Wolf?")

"That's irrelevant," I tell him. "That has nothing to do with this. I'm not leaving till I see him. I want five minutes. No more, no less."

It's now 12:30. I've been there since 9:30. He has not come out for lunch or even gone to the men's room. I'm sitting there on the sofa when he finally comes out. He's like a bull in the streets of

Pamplona. His face gets real red and he starts screaming. He puts his face right up to mine. All I can see is his red face. It was like an umpire going jaw to jaw with a ball player.

He's hollering into my face, and these are his exact words, over and over again: "You can't keep me a prisoner in my own office! You can't keep me a prisoner in my own office!" In my peripheral vision I see two eyeballs from every head on the twenty-fourth floor turn our way.

Calmly, I manage to say, "All I want is five minutes. I just want to know where I stand."

I don't think he heard what I said. "You can't do this!" he roars. "This is not the way to do business! I will not be forced into this!" On and on he goes, yelling, red-faced.

"I'm not forcing you," I say. "But all I want is five minutes." He turns away and walks out into the hall beyond the secretaries' desks. I'm standing there, kind of shell-shocked. No one's saying a word. A minute later he comes back and says, "All right, when do you want to get together?"

"At your convenience," I tell him.

He stands there looking at his secretary. She's showing him his appointment book. "All right," he says, "ten o'clock tomorrow morning. Be here then."

The next day, ten o'clock sharp, the door opens and he says, "Okay, come on in."

I told him I wanted to know where I stood. If he didn't want to give me any more major assignments, why carry the contract through? We could sign something right there letting me go free for the final nine months.

"Warner," he says, "I didn't know you haven't had any major assignments since last October. I'm going to have to talk to the senior producer. I don't know if you realize this, but he's the one in charge of handing out assignments. I'll see what I can do."

Well, between the time I saw him in June 1977 and March 1978, when my contract expired, I only did a third-string baseball game in August and a backup game in September. Plus I was taken off *College Football Scoreboard* that fall. I went from being a non-person to being an absolutely dead and buried person.

The odd thing about my meeting with him was for most of the hour we talked about *him*. He began telling me about his career.

"You know," he says, "I could've gone to CBS a few years ago. Could've gone to NBC. Got offers from all of 'em. They all wanted me. Even got an offer from Norman Lear. But I'm going to stay here, Warner. This is the place to be." For him it was, because he also became president of ABC-TV News and has done very well for the network. Looking back, although we didn't see eye to eye on my role at ABC, I must say I admire the man's work. He really is a genius in the business and he'll go down as one of the great innovators in television history.

15

The Corporate Game

Before I take you behind closed doors at ABC, I've got a story that shows how quickly your career can change in this business.

It's December 1977, six months after my confrontation with the president of ABC Sports. Without anybody knowing it except my wife and a few others, I had agreed to return to WTOP–Channel 9 in Washington. March 1978 is supposed to be my homecoming—the same month my ABC contract is due to expire in New York.

Meanwhile, the Post-Newsweek Company, the owner of WTOP, felt that it had to sell the station. It seemed the Federal Communications Commission was going to rule that companies could no longer own newspapers and broadcast stations in the same town. BOOM! That's it. "Sell the paper or sell the station," Post-Newsweek was told by the lawyers.

A short while later, my phone rings and it's Jim Snyder, my old boss at WTOP and one of the greatest bosses of all time. He says, "Warner, I've always been honest with you. I'm calling to tip you off. We are about to sell this place to the *Detroit Evening News*. So if you come back here, you wouldn't be working for me. You would be working for somebody else. Now I think you should still come back—you're still big in this town—but if you want out, I'm not going to hold you to your promise."

Wow, what an up-front guy! What a considerate thing to do. I said, "Jim, one of the reasons I was coming back was to get out of the kind of situation I'm in up here—and work for you. If I can't work for you, I might as well stay here with WABC locally.''

See? Life is strange, man. If the FCC had not threatened to impose that new rule, I'd probably have been in Washington the past five years.

Funny, but the *Washington Post* found out about my plans to come back and printed a story *after* my conversation with Snyder. ''Warner Wolf to Return to Channel 9,'' the headline read. But I had already spoken to Snyder, so it wasn't true any more. By the time somebody got to me for a comment, I honestly and correctly denied the story without having to say another word.

In March 1978, WABC gives me both the 6 and 11 o'clock shows, and I sign a brand new two-year contract with WABC to work exclusively for Channel 7. No more network affiliation, except for a clause which allowed the network to use me up to five events per year. They never did exercise that option. Now it's September 1979. I've been at Channel 7 three and a half years.

We are now the number one rated station in New York City and I have a pretty good following. I'm six months away from the expiration of my contract, and I want to start planning my future. Time to begin negotiations, right? WRONG! Apparently WABC higher-ups weren't as interested in extending our relationship as I was.

I go up to the general manager of Channel 7, a guy who had just come over from the ABC owned-and-operated station in Chicago.

I went up to him and said, ''All right, the contract expires in six months. What do you have in mind?'' He says, ''Meet me in the ABC executive dining room September twelfth.''

On September 12, I show up in the executive dining room. The general manager is there with the station news director. Bad news, man. The general manager begins by criticizing my work. He comes on heavy with sarcasm, trying to downgrade me. After a while, he finally makes an offer. I felt the offer should've been higher and reminded him I'd helped the station become number one.

You know the line the general manager comes up with? ''Ahhh, if you went to another station, you wouldn't affect the ratings that much.''

He was trying to downplay my value.

I said, ''Well, WCBS [Channel 2] is pretty close. I think I would help them be number one in six months.''

''Oh yeah? How about Channel 4 [WNBC]?'' he asked.

I said, ''Well, it would probably take a little longer.''

He then says, ''You are not worth what you are asking for.''

Now it's October 1979. I'm getting antsy. I've been trying to catch this guy for a whole month, even though we're in the same building. I'd see him on the elevator and he'd say, ''I don't have time to talk . . .'' I started getting suspicious. Were they going to dump me or what? At last I arranged a meeting for October 12 in the general manager's office. This time, I decide to bring my wife, Sue, along. I said, ''Look, hon, I want you to look this guy over because I don't want to be unfair. Who knows, maybe I'm misjudging the guy.''

Unbelievable, what happens. My wife is in the room and he starts using profane language. I believe he resented the fact that Sue was there and wanted to let her know he didn't think she belonged. Plus he knocks my half-hour World Series show which just aired. He says I had on too many guests. *Too many guests!* Come on, the fans loved the show. Phone calls, letters—they loved it. Old Dodgers, Giants, and Yankees. We had Dusty Rhodes, the hero of the '54 Series, we had Yogi Berra, who played in more World Series games than any other player, we had Phil Rizzuto, who is so popular in New York City that he could run for mayor and win, we had the late outstanding Elston Howard, perhaps the greatest versatile ball player in the history of the AL, and former Dodger pitcher Ralph Branca, whom we talked about earlier. It was a live show with an audience and the fans loved it . . . and all this guy could say was that we had too many guests. Maybe for him, but for any New York baseball fan, it was great. But you have to realize, this was all part of his bargaining tactic. He knew that part of what I wanted was a similar half-hour show on a regular basis, once a week during the fall and winter months. Well, despite these negative statements, I was still ready to lower my terms and make a deal right there. I really didn't want to leave the station. But he then says, "We'll get back to you in ten days."

You know when he got back to me? *January*. Didn't talk to me from October 12 to January, on a promise they'd be back in ten days. No letters, no contact, no nothing—and we're in the same building, only two floors apart. Plus I don't have an agent, so he couldn't say he contacted my agent. I figured, "Come on, man, this is ridiculous!" They were treating me like I'd never worked there. I mean I knew I was at least a little bit valuable.

Now right around the time all of this is going on, my wife and I are out getting bagels one Saturday night on 80th and Broadway and who should I run into but my old boss at Channel 7, my former news director Ron Tindiglia, who had since moved over to CBS. My wife saw him first—we were in our car and he was in the street with his wife, Misti, waving his arms for me to stop. So the four of us get into my car, eat bagels, and start to talk. Now Tindiglia had no idea of what was going on at Channel 7, so he says, "How's everything going?" I say, "You know, Ron, I tell you the truth, I'm not sure how everything is going." Then I proceed to tell him how the general manager is totally ignoring me.

"I can't believe it," Tindiglia says. "You want to talk to somebody from our station?" "Sure I'll talk to anyone," I tell him. A few days later, Neil Derrough, then the vice president and general manager of WCBS-TV, comes over to my apartment. After the meeting I say to Sue, "Gee, what a nice guy and a real gentleman. I wouldn't mind working for somebody like that." One month later, it's now November 1979, I meet Derrough again, along with Steve Cohen, the news director, and Peter Temple, the director of planning and finance. Again I think, "What up-front, class guys."

After the meeting, WCBS makes it clear that if and when I am legally free of my current contract with WABC, they would be interested in hiring me. Well, just to show you how fast news travels in this business, about a week later I get a call from Ron Kershaw, the news director at WNBC–Channel 4. We have dinner. Later, Kershaw, a real nice down-to-earth guy, arranges another meeting with me, himself, WNBC's general manager, Bob Howard, who used to be the president of the NBC network, Arthur Watson, president of NBC Sports, Bob Walsh, president of the five owned-and-operated NBC stations, and George Hiltzik, a top lawyer for NBC. We meet in a suite at the Dorset Hotel on 54th and Sixth. We discuss the same things I discussed with WCBS. The only difference is, they say if and when you are legally free from your present contract, we would also like to put you in the *network,* besides WNBC. Boy, another shot at the network. Man, was I flattered!

Now this was interesting to me. Here were the other major local stations in New York and a network willing to hire me when I'm free—but my own station, where I am employed, is telling me I'm not worth what I'm asking, even though my requests are exactly the same for all three stations.

Now all this time, I still have not heard a word from WABC. For all I know, considering their lack of interest, they might have been out hiring my replacement at that very moment.

(Just for the record, in the end it was a very difficult decision to make, choosing between WCBS and WNBC. Both are fine organizations and have good management. However, I felt my place was WCBS and have been very happy there.)

All right, it's now January 1980. Not *ten days* after my last meeting with the general manager, as he promised, but *three months later,* he finally calls me into his office, holding a piece of paper in his hand, and says, "Well, we're going to give you what you asked for. But first we have to take it to the ABC board of directors."

I said, "Don't take it to the board of directors. I'm not accepting it."

"Why?" he said.

"I'll tell you why. You had me, but you didn't contact me from October twelfth until now, even though you told me you would get back to me in ten days. For all I knew, you weren't interested. Now it's too late."

Now they really roll out the big guns. They invite me to a meeting with the president of ABC Television. Not just ABC Sports, but ABC Television. February 7, 1980. I brought along a copy of my letter of resignation, which I had given to the news director the day before, giving the company one month's formal notice. It was thirteen pages long. I wrote it out in longhand on WABC stationery. I said exactly what I had told the general manager—everything about not being used by ABC Sports, being taken off all the network shows, and getting the run-around when I brought up the question of a new contract with Channel 7.

When I got to the office of the president of ABC Television, not only was he waiting, but the head of the ABC owned-and-operated stations was also there. I have my letter of resignation in a manila envelope; I begin to pull it out and read it. All of a sudden the head of the O-and-O's starts waving his hand.

"Oh, no, no—that won't be necessary," he goes.

I say, "OK. As far as I'm concerned, I'll just tear it up. It's probably better that way anyhow. I don't want to condemn anybody. I'll just go ahead and tear it up."

As I'm ripping it up and throwing the pieces in the wastebasket, the president says to the head of the O-and-O's, "You sure you don't want to see this letter?"

"Nah, that's all right," the O-and-O boss says. "Let's get on with it." After a while, they begin talking about a new contract.

I say, "Gentlemen, thank you, but I am not changing my mind. When the contract expires, that's it."

The president of ABC Television and the president of the owned-and-operated stations wanted to have one more meeting the next day, so I invited them over to my apartment off Central Park West. I figured, if the pressure is gonna get this strong, at least I want to be on my turf, not theirs. All four of us—the president, the head of O-and-O's, Sue, and I—sit down in my living room.

"We're going to put you on the network again," the president says. "You want boxing? You've got boxing. You know that half-hour show you wanted to do for WABC at 7:30? You've got it."

"Too late," I tell 'em. "Plus you're telling me that I'll be working for the president of ABC Sports again. He has already taken me off three network shows—baseball, *Wide World*, and the scoreboard show."

"Oh, no, no!" the president says. "You misunderstand. He's your biggest fan. He loves you, Warner. He talks about you all the time. In fact, we're going to have him call you tonight."

I said, "Wait a minute. The only reason he would call me would be because you would ask him to call me."

That night I'm at the station, watching five games, preparing for the 11 p.m. news, and the phone rings. It's the president of ABC Sports.

PRESIDENT: Warner, maybe we misused you . . .

ME: Well, perhaps so, but you did take me off three shows and you chose not to use me in the 1980 Winter Olympics.

PRESIDENT: What three shows?

ME: *Monday Night Baseball*, host of *Wide World of Sports* and the *College Football Scoreboard*.

PRESIDENT: Yeah, I guess I did.

ME: Besides, the only reason you're calling me now is because the president of ABC Television asked you to call.

PRESIDENT: I knew you'd say that. I knew it. In fact, I told the president you'd say that.

Finally, word about my possibly going to WCBS or WNBC leaked out. Rumors were beginning to reach print. Vic Ziegel, formerly of the *New York Post,* had something about it in *New York* magazine.

Meanwhile, one of the most important months in TV, the May rating period, was approaching. Local stations live and die on the ratings they get that month. Why May? All I can tell you is that the ratings for this particular month help determine advertising rates for the rest of the year.

Now, there are two things you must know about a performer's contract. Number one, when the performer gets an offer from another station, the present station he works for has the right to match any other offer. And second, if the performer does decide to leave his present station when the contract expires, he must wait ninety days before appearing on the air in the same city at another station.

Less than two weeks after the meeting in my apartment, I called the president of the O-and-O's, who was vacationing in Sun Valley, Idaho. I said, "Listen, rather than me sitting out the ninety days, how about me working for you those ninety days and *then* I'll be free. It'll be good for you and good for me."

He says, "I'll talk it over with the legal department and I'll get back to you."

A few days later he calls me back and says it's a deal.

"OK," I tell him. "All I want is a piece of paper that says you'll release me in ninety days and that this in no way is an extension of the old contract."

So within a few days the ABC lawyers write it up and I sign it. February 22, 1980. It was a formal, official document on company stationery. The key sentence reads: "It is understood and agreed that on or after June 5, 1980, Warner Wolf may accept an offer of employment with any one of his choosing and immediately begin performing on-air services." That's it, I figure. Black and white language—a clear statement that ABC will not block me from going wherever I want when the ninety days are up.

Now it's May 5, 1980. I'm sitting in my office, preparing for the 6 p.m. show that evening. In walks this lawyer carrying an attaché case. He puts it down on my desk, opens the lid, pulls out this document, and sticks it in my hand.

"I'm serving you with papers," he says. "WABC and ABC are suing you for breach of contract."

"*Breach of contract?* What breach? What contract? Here's the contract!" I pull out the ninety-day agreement and show it to him.

He says, "I don't get involved in that. I'm just serving papers."

How do you like that? Suing *me* for breach of contract! They say I didn't give them a chance to match an outside offer. Come on, man, gimme a break! They had all the opportunity in the world to sign me from September to January, and they didn't do beans. And now, after it appears I may leave, they want to sue me, claiming that the reservation of rights clause in the February 22, 1980 agreement preserved their right to sue me for breach of contract.

16

The Trial: ABC vs. Warner Wolf

BOOM!

Judge Burton Sherman pounded his hammer in the courtroom every morning for four days, May 29 to June 3, 1980 excluding the weekend and Memorial Day. Although it wasn't easy going on the air each night at WABC after being on trial all day, it was something I had to do. It may sound corny, but when you are in show business, and television is show business, the show must go on. The guy at home watching you has his own problems, he doesn't want to hear about yours. If he turns on his set, you owe that person a performance. Now a few weeks before the trial, when we were taking the deposition in a lower court, I got the distinct impression that the lower court judge thought we should just sign with ABC for more money—settle out of court and it's all over. But that's not what we were looking for. By this time I had made up my mind I wanted to go to CBS.

As far as the trial itself goes, I have always felt that we were truly blessed having a trial judge who had an open mind, a sense of humor, and knew something about sports, and also two outstanding trial lawyers in Bob Callagy of New York City, who represented CBS, and my personal attorney from Chevy Chase, Maryland, Ivan Shefferman. Both men did their homework and presented their cases perfectly.

It turned out that one of the crucial points in the case was that WABC wasn't being completely honest. They had said, "If you stay with us these extra ninety days, we'll let you go and there will be no problem." Meanwhile, they were sending copies of their internal memos to an outside law firm, setting up their case against me. We showed in the trial that they knew as far back as February that they would use me on the air for the ninety days and *then* take me to court.

Of course, they claimed they had no intention of suing me at the time they signed the ninety-day deal in February. They said that only much later—long after the newspaper stories appeared—did they plan to sue.

Early in the trial, the WABC news director takes the stand. He tells the judge that back in February I told him that I had already had discussions with two other stations back in October and November. Still, the ABC lawyers are arguing that they had no idea where I would be going.

JUDGE SHERMAN: Now I take it from the salary Mr. Wolf was commanding, there are only certain other local stations he could work at throughout the United States at that salary scale, correct?

NEWS DIRECTOR: I know of no other market outside of New York . . .

JUDGE SHERMAN: Where in New York could he command that money besides ABC? Obviously CBS?

NEWS DIRECTOR: WABC, WCBS, WNBC, or perhaps one of the networks.

JUDGE SHERMAN: Well, conceivably he could work the network any place throughout the United States, but as far as local is concerned, it would have to be in the New York area to command that salary?

NEWS DIRECTOR: Just those three stations.

JUDGE SHERMAN: So, if he doesn't work for CBS and he doesn't work for you, then the only place left is NBC, is that correct?

NEWS DIRECTOR: I think that's probably a reasonable assumption.

JUDGE SHERMAN: Thank you very much. Let's take a recess.

The president of ABC Television takes the stand. While he's talking, Callagy, the CBS lawyer, produces the thirteen-page letter of resignation I ripped up and threw in the trash can on February 7. Incredible. Until the deposition the week before, I hadn't seen the letter since I ripped it up. Somehow it had been pieced together with Scotch Tape.

Now the judge fills in the blanks of what happened after I left the president's office that day.

JUDGE: You retrieved the letter?

PRESIDENT: Yes.

JUDGE: Out of the wastepaper basket?

PRESIDENT: I retrieved the letter, put it in an envelope and put it in my drawer.

Later, Callagy brings out the fact it may have been not one, but *two* ABC executives going into the trash can.

CALLAGY: Did you personally retrieve that letter from the wastebasket in your office?

PRESIDENT: It's either myself or the head of the O-and-O's. Probably both of us.

CALLAGY: Do you know how that exhibit came to be taped together?

PRESIDENT: When I learned of the lawsuit, I called our counsel and said I have this in my drawer, it's been sitting there, would you like to have it?

Now the interesting thing is that the head of the O-and-O's never took the stand. The same guy who arranged the ninety-day deal for me never shows up in the courtroom.

Third day of the trial, Callagy is cross-examining the chief corporate lawyer for ABC.

CALLAGY: Where is the head of the O-and-O's today?

ABC LAWYER: I don't know where he is today.

CALLAGY: Have you seen him?
ABC LAWYER: I saw him this morning.

Come on. He's one of the central figures in the case, but he never shows up. As a result, there seemed to be a conflict in ABC's testimony.

For example, I remember when the president of ABC Television was testifying. The questioning got around to the first meeting I had in September and October over a possible new contract. Remember, this is the time I was getting stonewalled by the general manager of WABC.

PRESIDENT: I authorized the head of the O-and-O's to make a deal when it was first brought to my attention, which was in middle fall.
JUDGE SHERMAN: And how much discretion did he have?
PRESIDENT: He had total discretion. . . . We had talked about the scope of the deal, Your Honor, and I said, "We have no alternative. Warner is very important to us. Sign him up."

But the point is they never did sign me up. Even in January, after ignoring me for three months, they told me they'd have to take it to the board of directors.

Either somebody dropped the ball by not following the president's orders to sign me, or apparently somebody was not being 100 percent truthful. Otherwise they would have offered me a contract like the president said he ordered back in the middle of fall.

Now, remember how I was going to have to sit out ninety days after my WABC contract expired on March 5? Well, in early February I signed a ninety-day *off the air* producers' agreement with WCBS. The idea was, instead of being unemployed for those ninety days, as soon as my WABC contract expired March 5, I would work behind the scenes at Channel 2. We felt it was all perfectly legal, because there was nothing in my WABC contract which prevented me from taking an *off the air* position. As long as I wasn't on the air, I could drive a cab, be a bartender, go on stage, or be a TV producer for those ninety days. Now, of course, when WABC signed me for those extra ninety days the ninety-day *off the air* agreement with WCBS naturally became null and void. However, WABC said it was illegal for me to sign any kind of agreement with WCBS until my contract with WABC expired.

Well, I'm happy to say, after one month of lawsuits, depositions, and a trial, Judge Sherman ruled in our favor, permitting me to go to work for Channel 2 immediately.

Here are Judge Sherman's exact words:

> "Wolf negotiated in good faith during the renegotiating period and before. If anything, plaintiff's [ABC's] constant delay and the downgrading of Wolf's abilities cast doubt on its good faith. . . .
>
> "ABC seeks, with the aid of this court, to require a reluctant Warner Wolf to work for it for two more years. The parties agree that there is no case in equity which ever forced a person, even a highly paid one, to work for another. . . .
>
> "It was not until receipt of his termination letter of February 5, 1980 that ABC began to take a zealous interest in his future. An inference can be drawn that the impetus for this new-found concern was the knowledge that Wolf was negotiating with arch-rival CBS. At the subsequent meeting he informed plaintiff that he 'had given his word' and 'had a gentleman's agreement,' and under no circumstances would he continue at ABC.
>
> "His grievances were well known. The inter-office memoranda indicate that on February 7, 1980, if not before, ABC was at least suspicious of Wolf's defection. There was also cloak-and-dagger activity by ABC across the war zone on Sixth Avenue to ascertain his future. . . .
>
> "The court finds as a fact that plaintiff [ABC] seeks

equity with unclean hands and excessively delayed in bringing this action.

"Wolf now asks, as he has on television, 'Gimme a break.' In these circumstances, equity can and the court shall.

"Mr. Wolf, you may now go to work for WCBS."

BOOM! Case dismissed!

That night, June 10, 1980, I went right on the air for Channel 2 and did the 11 p.m. sports, and I'm happy to say I've been doing the 6 p.m. and 11 p.m. sports ever since.

You might be interested to know that ABC brought its case to the appeals division of the New York County Supreme Court. But on July 10, 1980, the justices ruled 4–1 in my favor. Still not satisfied, ABC then went all the way to the State of New York Court of Appeals. On October 14, 1980, this court also ruled in my favor, by a 5–2 margin. Just for the record, although both appellate courts did rule in my favor, in all fairness to ABC, the courts disagreed with the trial court's ruling and held that I had breached my contractual obligations with ABC when I entered into the agreements with CBS in February 1980. As far as the network goes, I always felt that if somebody gave me the opportunity and let me be myself as they did in local, it would work. If my style works in New York and worked in Washington, D.C., for eleven years, why wouldn't it work in Philadelphia or Chicago or Boston? All it would take would be one progressive guy at the top to say OK, let's put him on.

Well, just to show you there is such a guy, in March 1982 I received a call from Van Gordon Sauter, the president of CBS News, who used to be president of CBS Sports. Mr. Sauter, along with Ed Joyce, the executive vice president of CBS News, and George Merlis, then the executive producer of the *Morning News*, asked me to be a regular each Friday morning at 7:45 a.m. on the *CBS Morning News*.

The greatest music to my ears occurred when Sauter, Joyce, and Merlis said, "Warner, we are putting you on the network because we want you to be yourself. We will not try to change you. We want to hear those BOOMS, SWISHES, LET'S GO TO THE VIDEOTAPE, and GIMME A BREAK! We are hiring what we see every night in New York on WCBS-TV.''

After all those years, I finally met a network executive who was not afraid to let me be myself. He truly did ''Give me a break.''

Epilogue

Whenever I am invited to go around to groups and discuss sports, one question usually pops up. Somebody will ask, "Hey, Warner, besides working your way up the ladder from the smaller stations, what's your key to success?"

Well, the first thing, *you've got to have a positive attitude*. Have you ever noticed how many people walk around grumbling? Go to lunch with them and everything is down, like the world is coming to an end. Negative this, negative that. Complain here, complain there. Hey, forget that. I don't say you have to deny reality, but you're going to fail if you keep thinking how miserable everything is.

Second, *you've got to avoid office politics*. Don't listen to gossip, and don't get involved in it. Concentrate on your work, and not on office intrigue. I've seen a lot of guys who could have been great newsmen or sportscasters if they didn't waste so much of their time concentrating on who was doing what to whom.

Third is to *be prepared*. There's no shortcut to success. It's unbelievable how many guys don't do their homework. My father used to say there is no such thing as luck. "Luck is when preparation meets opportunity," he said. I think that's 100 percent right.

Fourth, *get some humor in your life*. It's related to a positive attitude. Too many people go around sourpuss. Come on, smile. Find the humor. There can be something funny in almost everything.

And there's usually something funny in what *you* do. It goes back to laughing at yourself. If you can't laugh at yourself, you don't have the right to laugh at anyone else.

And, fifth is *belief in God*. To me, there is no question that God gave me the tools and ability to do this kind of work. Without God, I would be lost. I also realize that God can remove those tools and the ability any time He wishes. I just thank God He has blessed my life. You can try it without God, but it's a heck of a lot easier *with* Him.

Index

ABOUT THE AUTHOR

Warner Wolf, television sportscaster, is in his fourth year as the regular week-night sports commentator for WCBS-TV in New York, Channel 2, and also appears weekly on Friday mornings, on the *CBS Morning News*. He has made his mark on the industry by vastly expanding the use of videotape highlights of sports. Before WCBS, Mr. Wolf was sportscaster for ABC on *Wide World of Sports*, *Monday Night Baseball*, and the 1976 Winter and Summer Olympics, as well as WABC-TV in New York.

Mr. Wolf began his career in 1961 with WLSI radio in Pikeville, Kentucky, before moving on to WEPM radio, Martinsburg, West Virginia; WQMR radio, Silver Spring, Maryland; and WTOP radio and television, Washington, D.C. Known as "Mr. Sports" in Washington, he covered all the major sports events for WTOP-TV and did play-by-play for the Washington Redskins, Senators, and Bullets. Warner has the distinction of having been three times named Sportscaster of the Year by the National Association of Sportscasters and Sportswriters, and was also named to *Who's Who* in 1983.